THE QUALITY OF MERCY

The quality of mercy is not strained.

Merchant of Venice, Act IV, sc 2.

"Woman, has no one condemned you?
Neither do I condemn you.
Go, and from now on do not sin again."

cf John 8:10-11

John Arnold

The quality
of mercy

A fresh look at
the Sacrament of Reconciliation

Foreword by
Cardinal Basil Hume osb

ST PAULS

ST PAULS Publishing
Morpeth Terrace, London SW1P 1EP, U.K.

Copyright © ST PAULS 1993

ISBN 085439 433 8
First published 1993. Reprinted 1999.

Set by TuKan, High Wycombe
Produced in the EC
Printed by The Guernsey Press Co. Ltd, C.I.

St Pauls is an activity of the priests and brothers
of the Society of St Paul who proclaim the Gospel
through the media of social communication

Contents

Foreword

Westminster Cathedral has a long tradition in providing for the celebration of the Sacrament of Reconciliation for which I know large numbers of people continue to be grateful. It was a service to the Catholic community commended by the Holy Father during his visit in 1982. It is appropriate that this book comes from a chaplain at the Cathedral and I welcome the invitation that it makes to reflect on the importance that this sacrament can have for each one of us.

The sacraments are such vital gifts for the life of the Church and we must be prepared to question and develop our own understanding of them so that their full value may be appreciated, and celebrated. This is particularly true in the Sacrament of Reconciliation which confers considerable freedom so that each individual may draw the greatest personal benefit. Whilst the years since Vatican II have seen developments in our theological understanding of this sacrament, I suspect that not enough has been said about how we should set about using it well or to consider why so many people apparently no longer choose to use it at all. This book offers a guide and helps to ask the questions that we should all be addressing about our personal use of the sacrament. It reminds us of the first and most important element of God's love for us and the expression of that love through forgiveness and encouragement.

I recommend this book to you in the hope that it will instil a new sense of gratitude for that quality of mercy which is not strained.

Archbishop of Westminster

ACKNOWLEDGEMENTS: This little book only exists because of the encouragement received from many people; far too many to mention by name. Three names must stand for all, but that does not diminish the sincere gratitude that I owe to those not named here who gently pestered and cajoled me at various points along the way and who gave such practical and invaluable help so generously. To Clare Barbour my thanks for the original idea and enthusiasm that prompted seven short articles for the *Westminster Cathedral Bulletin* and later for a small pamphlet, to Jane Milward for the expertise of editing and for providing a discipline of manageable deadlines that produced the completed text and to Anne-Marie McGovern for so much of the word-processing. From among many others, my thanks to the chaplains at Westminster Cathedral and brother priests who have helped me to develop a clearer understanding of the power of this sacrament.

Introduction

One of the most pronounced characteristics of his Father's love that Jesus emphasises, and which is presented in the gospels, is that of forgiveness. Time and again Jesus portrays both the Father's determined willingness to forgive and our need to be forgiven. It is indeed the perfection of love in God that makes forgiveness such a vital part of his self-revelation. Because God loves, therefore he forgives. Because God is love, he is forgiveness. To reason this in any other way would make nonsense of the fact that God's love is perfect. Love which fails to forgive or which puts a limit or condition on forgiveness is not a real love at all. Our human love fails because we often reach a point at which we feel unable to forgive, but that is our human weakness. Perfect love demands perfect forgiveness – a forgiveness which cannot be exhausted, which cannot be limited. The most specific forum, though by no means the exclusive one, by which that same forgiveness is conferred in our own time is in the Sacrament of Reconciliation.

In the pages which follow, we shall be reflecting on the use and practice of the Sacrament of Reconciliation and considering whether the qualities that Jesus demonstrated in the gospels are adequately represented in our present usage, and where we might need to radically rethink our image of God and our understanding of sin and discipleship.

It is of vital importance that the power which Jesus invested in the sacrament should not be lost through ignorance or complacency, or neglect. Familiarity, we are told, breeds contempt. Could it be that we have become so familiar with it, that we now fail to see past the rituals of prayers and place to glimpse the true purpose of what is happening in the celebration of this sacrament? Have we lost something of its power, or did we never really learn its value? History and the passing of time may so easily dull the full significance of what Jesus was teaching, and it is for every generation to reflect on the fulness of Christ's teaching and be sure to make a renewal of life which retains the power of what he taught us. Tradition helps us to preserve the ministry of Christ, but tradition may lose its immediacy if it is merely transmitted from one generation to another. For example, the parables that Jesus employed provided familiar images by which he could teach the people about God through elements that were used in everyday life. So much of the strength of a parable may be lost by seeking to apply it in different places and times where the richness of the symbols are unappreciated, because they are not familiar to people in the way that they were to the crowds who listened to Jesus. And where the power and the urgency of what Jesus said has been diluted, it must be re-discovered.

A person's relationship with God is personal. It certainly has a public dimension in the community, since we are all parts of one body – the Church. If our community is healthy, then we will receive much encouragement and help; but in the end our relationship with God is our own which must be personally renewed if it is to be mature. Just as baptismal promises and marriage vows benefit from such renewal, so our use of the Sacrament of Reconciliation will surely benefit from reflection and self-questioning. If the following pages prompt such consideration, or encourage a fresh look, they will have achieved their main purpose.

This book has also been written because so little is ever said about the Sacrament of Reconciliation. Most of us learn how to go to confession when we are very small, about seven years of age. Once that learning is complete, nothing is said about the sacrament again. Certainly, there may be reminders that certain seasons of the year, like Advent and Lent, are particularly appropriate times to go to confession, but I have heard almost nothing about 'how' to go to confession. The consequence of this is that the individual's ability to use the sacrament is choked. Remember one of the subjects that you learned at school and gave up at, say, sixteen years of age. Because that subject has not been developed, your knowledge of it has stagnated. Not only have you not learned more about it, but it is doubtful that you remember more than the basics of what it was all about.

This is rather what has happened for most of us with the sacrament. We learned about the sacrament, but we never extended our knowledge, and it has become trapped in the world of our childhood. We did not get any encouragement to develop it as we grew to adulthood. No wonder so many people have come to regard the sacrament as irrelevant – in the form as it is. How often I have heard the confessions of mature, professional, committed people, but their confessions were those of children.

What is written here is meant as an invitation to reflect on and to develop the practice of celebrating this sacrament, and I am particularly remembering a number of different people. First, I am thinking of persons received into the Catholic Church as adults. Secondly, there are those who find confession a chore, an observance, to be honoured with acceptable frequency but with little apparent benefit. Thirdly, I have in mind those who came to the conclusion that confession was of no relevance and who abandoned its practice. Finally, this is written for those people who have heard that Catholics have to 'go to confession', and are curious to know what it is all about and whether the more bizarre things that they have heard about it are true.

By reason of my appointment to Westminster Cathedral, where there are sixty hours of confessions each week, I have had to question my attitude to the sacrament in the light of my experience. While I have come to have a profound respect for it, I am saddened by the apparent misunderstanding and mistrust that surround it. These pages are partly the fruit of that personal experience, and partly the product of a firm belief that the sacrament is at present a wasted sacrament, the meaning of which needs to be renewed and re-discovered. Somewhere in its history and practice its profound meaning has been lost or at least forgotten. The overwhelming generosity of God's loving forgiveness has been tragically disguised, quite unintentionally, behind formulas and rules and a monotony of practice.

PART 1

New beginnings

Chapter 1

Recognising the dilemma

'Bless me, Father, for I have sinned. It is six months since my last confession. I have missed Mass on one Sunday, but that is my only mortal sin. I have told lies. I have been uncharitable. For these sins and the sins of all my past life I am truly sorry and beg pardon and absolution from you, my spiritual father.'

Is this brief example of a confession familiar to you? It is certainly familiar to me, both as the sort of confession that I was taught to make and one which reflects many of the confessions that I now hear as a priest. It is so familiar, in fact, that it seems to be a formula which has been learned by heart by thousands of people, and which is recited over and over again, with some minor variations.

'Three years, Father, so obviously I have not made my Easter duties. I have been angry. I have not said my morning and night prayers. I have stolen. I have had impure thoughts. That is all.'

I would not doubt the good intentions of a person who speaks in this way. Their presence in the confessional at all pre-supposes a genuine desire to receive forgiveness. But in both these examples the reality and the true meaning of the sacrament have been undermined by a routine and a formula so that its full value has been disguised, if not lost.

We will look carefully at these formulas in due course, but I would like to suggest one or two guidelines which should be part of our use of the sacrament.

When we come to celebrate the Sacrament of Reconciliation we are bringing our own experience, which is unique. It is a privileged moment when we have the freedom to reflect on who we are and what has gone wrong, while putting it into the context of the circumstances of our life.

I ought to admit that I never found 'going to confession' easy or pleasant. For some years at school, it was a valued excuse to get away from a period of private study in the classroom and to wander through the school to the chapel. My confession was always more or less the same, not entirely irrelevant but a long way short of reflecting my life as it actually was. Then there was a period when I went to the sacrament out of habit. During my studies for the priesthood, I should think that the use (I can hardly call it celebration) of the sacrament must have registered my frustration and despondency that I was not as good a person as I wanted to be, and a long way from living the perfection to which we are called in the Gospel.

As a priest, the gap between what I am and what I would want to be remains as irritatingly wide as ever. But my attitude to the sacrament has changed considerably. It now represents a time when I can be honest with myself, off-loading things that weigh on my conscience, and a moment where I can put my spiritual house back in order. It allows me the opportunity to experience the inexhaustible love of God who is prepared – in fact, longing – to forgive me yet again, and to encourage me to start again. I will not say that all the awkwardness of admitting what is wrong has gone, or that I necessarily enjoy the sacrament. In fact I find it hard work; but I know how much I now value the opportunity it gives me and the power and generosity of God which it demonstrates.

Let us return to those two examples of confession. They may well be full of the best intentions, but they demonstrate a very naive and unhelpful knowledge of the sacrament and they suggest a very unhealthy attitude to God.

Perhaps the saddest thing about them is the fact that they are formulas. The words have been learned by heart by the speaker, to be repeated as and when required, without thought. The content of these confessions does not reflect the reality of the individuals' lives because they say nothing about the person. These 'shopping lists' are of little or no value when it comes to learning about a person, nor do they help the individual to recognise what is wrong in his or her life, what needs forgiveness and what needs help. Nearly everything that is said is vague and general. Apart from the mention of a failure to attend Mass on one occasion, everything else is couched in vague generalities which could mean a variety of different things, and in some cases there is no sin or fault at all.

The first penitent speaks of having missed Mass and of that being a mortal sin. The old catechisms told us that to miss Mass was indeed a mortal sin; but it is clear that a sin (in the language of those same catechisms), to be mortal, must be grave matter and committed with full knowledge and full consent. Time and time again, I have found that the penitent has indeed missed Mass but for perfectly adequate reasons: that he had been travelling in a place where there were no churches, or he had been ill, or looking after someone else who was ill.

The statements that a person has told lies and stolen are unhelpful unless there are also some further indications about the damage that might have been intended or done by the lie, or the value of the thing stolen and the motive for stealing it. Stealing a couple of envelopes from work would rank rather differently from stealing a week's pension from someone who would have no other resources on which to live.

There is no sin at all in failing to say morning and night prayers. Certainly we are called to pray, and St Paul tells us to pray without ceasing, but there is no hard and fast method of prayer which must be observed by all. Prayer may be entered into at any time, best suited to the individual, and in a variety of ways. If morning and evening are suitable, then that is fine; but there is an invitation to pray at any time, and to remain prayerful and conscious of the presence of God at all times. Indeed, an attitude that prayers need to be said in the morning and evening may betray a mechanical approach to prayer which, like confession, has become a matter of the repetition of formulas for the penitent.

How much more constructive it would be to be able to recognise that 'I have not spent enough (or perhaps, any) time with God in prayer', and to know that life has been the less fulfilling for that lack of prayer. To think that a healthy prayer life consists of a formula of prayer first thing in the morning and last thing at night seems almost to suggest that there is no need or purpose in trying to live in the presence of God at all times, and to see Christ as the centre and the inspiration for all that we do and say. Of course, the offering of the day to Almighty God as we begin the day, and drawing everything together in prayer at the end of the day are good practices, but not essential or to be treated as adequate.

As for the matter of Easter duties, we must tread with care. Many people still believe that there is an obligation to receive absolution and communion within the Easter season. This was the case when the reception of communion was very rare, and absolution was required before each occasion. When Pope Pius X invited everyone, even small children, to receive communion frequently, the requirement to go to confession each time became both impracticable and without justification and was no longer insisted upon. Catholics are still obliged to receive communion at least once a year, and the most appropriate time for doing this would be thought to be during the Easter season unless it is received at some other time for a particular reason. Members of the Church are bound to go to the Sacrament of Reconciliation at least once a year where there is serious sin in need of forgiveness – the season in which that is done is of no consequence. So often in confession, people say things which show that they do not know what is required of them, that they are not clear what sin is and what it is not, and this necessarily frustrates their proper use of the sacrament.

Our penitents have also spoken of anger and lack of charity. Anger may be destructive and it may be wrong, but that is not necessarily the case, for anger may also be justified and be quite the correct response in the circumstances. Jesus himself was angry with the money-changers and stall-keepers in the Temple and he was right to be angry. We may all be angry when we see injustice. The anger itself is not a sin, but the circumstances in which it occurs and the way in which it is or is not controlled may well be sinful. These are things which must be reflected upon if the real nature of the fault or failing is to be established.

Much the same must also apply to any confession of being uncharitable. Charity, or love, is the heart of the whole Gospel message, the centre of Christ's teaching. To say that I have not been charitable is to say everything and nothing. To be of value in the confession such a statement surely needs better definition. How have I been uncharitable? Perhaps I have been irresponsible or negligent. Perhaps I have been cruel to someone by taunting them or ignoring them. All this process of reflection and self-realisation will be dealt with at greater length in Chapter 5. Weighing our faults must be an essential ingredient when it comes to using the sacrament well.

Also included in our brief confessions were 'impure thoughts'. These are usually, but not always, concerned with sexual matters. Sexuality is at one and the same time both the taboo subject and the bogey-man, which individuals so often find too embarrassing to discuss or consider, even within the confidentiality of the confessional. For many people, sexuality has been made a problem. Whether or not that has ever been the case, the Church has often been 'perceived' as regarding sex and everything associated with it as something dirty and sinful. But this is far from the truth. The teachings of the Church are clear in emphasising the beauty and importance of sexuality. It is a wonderful gift and, like all things that are precious, it is easily damaged and can be badly misused. We should

19

rejoice in our sexuality and recognise it as a very precious gift. Perhaps it is just a question of our nervousness or embarrassment, but sex has too often been made a taboo subject and within the secrecy we manage to create feelings of guilt. That is not to say that matters of sex need to be openly discussed or flaunted, though our 'tabloid society' seems often to think of little else. Our sexuality is something that is private, but not something that needs to be hidden.

What is sexuality? It is a gift from God that enables us to love others and, appropriately, to give ourselves to one other person, in a life-long commitment, in the Sacrament of Marriage. Our tradition teaches us that sexuality is only complete in its expression when a man and a woman have given themselves to each other in this sacrament. But because our sexuality is so much a part of us, it expresses itself both rightly and wrongly in much more of our lives; it is not something that simply appears in the lives of married people. We need to learn how we may best embrace this great gift, but because it emerges during adolescence and early adulthood – and is very often something for which an individual has not been prepared – learning may well occur through mistakes and confusion.

Therefore, our sexuality may well be something that we will need to speak about in our confession; and it is a pity that it is so often spoken about in a sense of guilt and shame, and hidden behind hopelessly general words and phrases, all of which sound so negative, such as 'impure thoughts', 'abuse' and 'lusting'. Living with our sexuality does not mean that we cannot find others both beautiful and attractive – indeed we should do so for that is the way that God has made them – but it does mean that we should always esteem the dignity of such people and not demean them by our thoughts and behaviour.

Enjoying our sexuality is not an alternative to our attempts to love God. We are sexual beings because it is part of all that God has given to us. Disciplining that sexuality will not necessarily be easy, particularly in a society which seems to be obsessed with popular notions about sexual behaviour and so-called 'sexual freedom'. Our merging of our sexuality with all that we are, as individuals loved by God, calls on us to arrive at standards constantly demanded of those who would follow Christ.

It is so important that we discover and cherish the beauty of our sexuality, and avoid that destructive notion that sexuality is something that needs to be hidden and suppressed because it is wrong. There is no doubt that it is one of the sources of scruples and guilt, an endless worry, when in fact it should be the source of celebration and thanksgiving.

Confessing 'impure thoughts' is of little help either to priest or penitent, and indeed may represent no real fault at all but merely the disclosure of perfectly legitimate and healthy sexual feelings.

Finally, our first penitent used a formula to close his confession which speaks of including all the sins of his past life. This phrase is so often used, but it suggests that the penitent has mistaken what absolution means in the Sacrament of Reconciliation. And what is rather more worrying, this misunderstanding may leave the penitent open to the crippling fear of scrupulosity and the all too common and unhealthy burden of negative guilt.

If we are to use the Sacrament of Reconciliation well, and if it is to become a celebration in our lives rather than an unpleasant but necessary observance, then it is vital that we correct fundamental misconceptions and come to understand the value and the generosity of God's gift to us in the sacrament.

The penitent who carries his or her guilt from one confession to another, needing to remind God that there are still feelings of guilt from the past, has not understood the basic truth that when God forgives, his forgiveness is complete and perfect; it is as if those faults and sins of the past had never occurred. When we come to the sacrament and ask for forgiveness of our God, who is perfect love, then we must believe that the forgiveness that we receive is not that human sort of forgiveness which so often hangs on to the offences of the past; not really forgiving a person for what has gone wrong but only giving that person permission to carry on, with the fault remaining a memory. We probably find it very difficult to believe that God has forgiven us because we have only experienced that sort of human – and incomplete – forgiveness that leaves the memory of the wrong in our own and other people's minds, all too readily available to be revived at some moment in the future.

If your confession sounds remotely like either of the above examples, then what is written here is intended for you. It is an invitation to bring your understanding and use of the sacrament more into line with the person you are. The Sacrament of Reconciliation is about a great deal more than simply getting our sins forgiven. It is concerned with our relationship with God, and with one another, with our place and dignity as individuals within the community of the Church. More than just confessing our sins, we are getting in touch with who we are and what the Christian pilgrimage through life means and the direction it indicates to us all. It seems to me to be essential that we learn to use the sacraments in the way that Christ intended that we should. If we have got trapped because of a lack of education or reflection, then we must confront the inadequacies.

If you have abandoned the use of the sacrament, you might have done so for a number of reasons. Perhaps you think that it has become irrelevant precisely because it does not allow you to express yourself, as you are. Perhaps you feel that what you say in the confessional may have nothing to do with the way you live your life, the concerns that you have and the sorts of decisions that you must make. It could equally, and tragically, be because you have had a bad experience of the sacrament; either because what you said was misunderstood or because you came across a priest who was aggressive or lacking in sympathy and understanding.

Hopefully, there will be something in what is written here for new Catholics; those who have been received into the Church as adults and who are learning about the sacraments and their application to daily life. Most individuals who now actively seek to be members of the Catholic Church are asked to commit themselves to a period of instruction with a group, following a cycle of learning and discussion which is called the Rite of Christian Initiation of Adults. There is plenty of time for discussion on any theme, but there is still the moment when, having been received into the Church, the individual must begin to put into practice what has been learned and recognise that there will always be much more which must be understood, developed and renewed.

Finally, these thoughts and reflections are also intended for those who are not Catholics but who are either suspicious or just curious of what is meant by 'confession'. Confession has probably attracted more comment and mythology than almost any other aspect of Catholic traditions, and there is certainly a lot of useful 'demythologising' that should be done for this sacrament to be understood for what it is.

As we begin our own study of this sacrament, we do so in the knowledge that it has lost a great deal of its appeal. There is nothing wrong in various religious practices being, for a time, more or less popular. But in the case of the Sacrament of Reconciliation, there seems to be something badly amiss. There has definitely been a sharp decline in the numbers of people who actually go to confession. This apparently is not simply that individuals go less often, but that large numbers of people no longer go at all. This again would not be of major concern except that we are not speaking of a pious practice but of a sacrament of the Church. There are only seven sacraments and these are particular and profound moments in which God touches our lives. Only two of the seven are available for frequent, repeated reception – the Eucharist and Reconciliation. That either of these two should suffer a slump in attendance should be a major concern because a means by which God, through Christ, has chosen to work in the Church, is being ignored. When we know our frailty as human beings, we must surely become aware of our need to call on God's help and assistance whenever it is available, for without him we can do nothing (cf Jn 17).

We would of course be right to say that the Eucharist has also suffered a decline. In the last thirty years, for a wide variety of reasons, many Catholics have either left the Church completely or ceased to attend Mass and receive communion on such a regular basis as before. That obviously has its sadness and its disappointment; but within our understanding of the problem we can at least now see that the decline has levelled out and, in some cases, there is the encouragement of revival.

The problem facing the Sacrament of Reconciliation goes deeper. The decline has outstripped the number of those who have left the Church. It indicates that many who practise their faith no longer include this sacrament as part of that practice. The days are gone, in most countries, when confessions were a regular feature of the pastoral ministry of every parish church. Even where time is still allocated every week for confessions, most priests would say that the long lines of penitents have been drastically reduced.

There seem to be only three instances where the practice of the sacrament remains consistent or is on the increase. The first, and most difficult one to quantify, is in the field of spiritual direction and retreats. A growing number of Catholics have spiritual directors whom they visit on a regular basis, or they avail themselves of the opportunity of confession while making a retreat; a practice that has grown enormously in popularity within the last twenty years or so.

Secondly, the city centre parishes and cathedrals have maintained larger numbers of penitents. This would seem to suggest that many people prefer to use this sacrament when their identity is unknown and where that anonymity is all but guaranteed. A question or two needs to be asked as to the reasons for this. Is it simply a question of embarrassment at confessing to a priest who is familiar to us or by whom we are known? Is it a lack of trust in or knowledge of the confidential seal of the confessional? These are questions which we need to address. The 'seal' of the sacrament requires that a priest never, for whatever reason, reveals anything that a penitent has said in the confessional, nor may he imply what he has heard through his speech and behaviour to others. It is one of the strictest requirements of secrecy to be found anywhere in our world, and one which the priest regards as very precious within his ministry. Those who go to confession need to have the greatest confidence that what is spoken is done so without any danger that information will be passed to others. Penitents are not bound in the same way; they may speak to others both about what they have said and about anything the priest has said, but this is not so in the case of the priest, who must be silent. This requirement of secrecy is also laid on those who may overhear anything that is said in the confessional and on a person who might have been required, through necessity, to be present as an interpreter between priest and penitent.

It is on the integrity of this seal that so much of the value of this sacrament resides. People must be able to speak without any fear of what they have said being repeated. Canon law requires the highest standards of the priest, and imposes heavy penalties on those who compromise the standard required of them.

The third instance where the sacrament has maintained, and indeed increased in, its popularity is in the Reconciliation Services or Penitential Services which are normally held in parishes during Lent and Advent. These services comprise a whole liturgy, the theme of which is that of repentance and forgiveness. The services often include the opportunity for individual confessions, though sometimes a 'general absolution' is conferred, which is generally discouraged or disallowed by the bishops and by the canon law of the Church. The popularity of these services may depend on a desire for a more prepared and considered celebration of the sacrament, which is to be welcomed, or a determination to celebrate something of the sacrament without the need to attend the sacrament individually.

Chapter 2

Historical influences on the sacrament

It would not be an easy or a very realistic task to give a detailed account of the history of this sacrament here. The present form of the sacrament was not established until the twelfth century, and yet the most important elements which make up its celebration are identifiable from the earliest records of the Jewish nation. Therefore, it would not serve any great purpose to attempt a history in the normal sense of the word. It would be more useful to select influences that have been of particular importance. Then we would better understand how the Sacrament of Reconciliation has arrived at its present form. We would also need to know how those elements may now be best employed. That would help us in establishing the most fruitful use of the sacrament.

Jesus instituted seven sacraments. This is a truth of our faith which was declared by the Council of Trent. But while there is an attractive simplicity in establishing that Jesus is the author of the Sacrament of Reconciliation, we cannot point to any particular event in the ministry of Jesus when he told his disciples that he was instituting the sacrament and that it was to have certain elements which were necessary for its validity. We must look more carefully at the context in which Jesus was teaching to understand more fully what he intended to establish in the sacramental life of the Church. Indeed, when we talk of Jesus 'instituting' seven sacraments, we by no means intend to declare that Jesus wanted the life of the Church to be structured around seven specific events. What we do mean is that from the ministry of Jesus may be drawn seven life-giving moments which are part of the life of the members of the Church. Obviously, it is easy to see where the Eucharist was enacted for the first time, at the last supper, but this is not as clear for other sacraments, such as the Anointing of the Sick or Ordination.

Before his ministry began, Jesus was a disciple of the Jewish law. He studied the history and tradition of the people that God had chosen as his own. He was familiar with the precepts of the Torah, the Jewish law, and all the books of the Scriptures that recounted the experience of the Jewish people. Those laws and traditions were to be maintained and completed by the ministry of Christ – something that he guaranteed in his own words.

Within that history of the Jewish nation, forgiveness had forged a most important role. The whole of that history was the story of the relationship between God and his people which had been sealed in the covenant, a contract of fidelity which bound them together. By the covenant, the people declared their obedience and dedication to the One Lord God and in return he promised a fidelity to and protection of his people, whom he would guide in truth and prosperity. But there were many occasions when the people were not faithful to their promise, when they failed to honour God, when they worshipped other gods, or broke the law which had been given to them.

There are numerous examples of the breaking of this covenant. In every case, it was restored. Often that restoration only came after God had shown his anger and where he had punished the people, but a new covenant was always eventually established. A most important fact in this event of reconciliation was that the covenant was not simply repaired, but it was allowed to mature. The covenant grew stronger. Reconciliation did not merely wipe out the misdeeds of the people, but it heralded a new relationship with God which was to be that much stronger; God drawing the people a little closer to himself. That is a most important element which we must recall when we discuss our own use of the Sacrament of Reconciliation.

Probably the best example of this occurred at the time of the exile of the Jews in Babylon. God had been angry with them for their disobedience and for the way that they had failed to maintain any real allegiance to their God or to worship him with sincerity. Despite the warnings of the prophets, they continued their poor behaviour and a political disaster overtook them. The Temple in Jerusalem was destroyed by the armies of the Babylonian Empire and the cream of the Jewish nation, its scholars, priests and rulers were deported to Babylon, leaving Jerusalem a desolate city.

It was by God's initiative that the punishment came to an end after about seventy years. God began the process of re-establishing the covenant and reconciling himself with his people. He sent the prophet Ezekiel to explain how the relationship between God and his people would be mended, but Ezekiel spoke in terms which showed that, with the new covenant, God was to be even closer to his people. He was to breathe his own life into them, washing them clean and putting his own spirit in their hearts. God had never spoken to his people in such a way before; the new covenant did not simply restore the relationship that had existed before, but it created a new and closer union.

To this often-repeated experience in the Old Testament, with which Jesus would have been very familiar, must be added the role of John the Baptist which was of particular importance, for two reasons. John was the herald of the Messiah. He was to proclaim the imminent coming of Jesus as the Messiah, the one for whom all the people were waiting, the one who would set Israel free and through whom a definitive and final covenant was to be made with God. In that sense, John was to close that period of Israel's history when the people drew closer to God, by announcing the coming of the One who would make the lasting covenant. The expectation of the Jewish people was that the Messiah would have a political and social role; freeing Israel from the oppressive occupation of the Roman Empire and restoring its former dignity. Jesus, as we now know, was not intending to take up that sort of role at all, but wished rather to be concerned with the spiritual life of the people. Whilst announcing a new and final stage in the history of the covenant, John introduced a new element in the idea of covenant. Throughout the history of the covenant, God had dealt with a whole nation, a single corporate identity. Of course there had been many individuals who had played specific roles during its history, but the covenant had always been a relationship between God and the whole people. John introduced a new element of individuality, calling each person to repentance rather than appealing just to a national identity.

A sense of sinfulness and a need to be forgiven formed a strong part of the liturgy of the Jews. For the Feast of the Atonement, for example, the people did penance and fasted because of their sins, which they symbolically loaded onto a goat. It was driven into the desert as a sign of the people's determination to be rid of their sinful past and to drive evil away. Forgiveness was sought constantly in prayer, especially in the recitation of the psalms, many of which have a strong sense of repentance and renewal.

The need for repentance and the desire for forgiveness were already, therefore, important parts of the faith and tradition of the Jewish people when Jesus began his own ministry. This is not the place to give a detailed account of Christ's ministry. We shall be drawing on many texts in later chapters. But it is essential to see that forgiveness was at the very root of his work and the reason for so many of the actions that we see recorded in the gospels. His forgiveness was lavish, free and complete, without sanction and even given sometimes without a request for it being made. The full quality of his forgiveness must be clearly understood. Since Christ is the Son of God and the perfect image of the Father, we see in the way Christ forgives a reflection of the way God longs to forgive. And when Christ commissioned us, through the disciples, to carry on his mission, he commissioned us to preserve and to proclaim that same quality of forgiveness in the Church throughout all ages.

This sense of mission needs to be clearly understood. It is by the very fact of our Baptism that we are commissioned to carry on the work that Christ had begun but which had been necessarily left unfinished by his death. He came to teach us about his Father, to remind us of the greatest commandment of the law, and to show us how that commandment could be lived. To be Christian, to be Christ's disciple, is not just to accept what he taught but to live as he did and to minister to those in need, just as he had done. That ministry was not something that was passive, avoiding what was wrong, but filled with the unpredictable activity of responding to the needs of others. Our purpose must be to re-discover the potential of that forgiveness and to live in a relationship with God and with one another which reflects the quality of forgiveness that God has revealed to us.

Tracing the role of forgiveness and the sense of reconciliation which Jesus had so willingly offered is not easy as we enter into the early centuries of the Church's history. Outside elements had a strong bearing on the understanding that people had of the forgiveness of God. Dominating the religious atmosphere in that first generation after the resurrection of the Lord was the keen belief that his promise to return would soon be fulfilled. There was an urgency with which individuals were received into the Church community and a strictness with which they held themselves 'in waiting' for Christ's second coming.

It is also important to remember that the Church did not grow in a unified and uniformly-structured way. Growth was fast but communities grew in isolation from one another. We tend to forget that, while the Pax Romana allowed for a certain degree of safety in travel, distances were long and communication difficult. Having accepted the fundamental truths of belief in Christ, each community structured itself according to its own culture, meeting its everyday needs in the light of its new faith. The Letters of St Paul give us a most useful insight into the diversity of cultures that he encountered in his missionary journeys. He writes to different communities about their own particular problems, many of which were born of the fact that each community received the Good News of Christ against varying backgrounds of pagan traditions. This led to a considerable diversity within the early Church, which was reflected in the worship and community life. In the matter of forgiveness and reconciliation with God, while all communities acknowledged the forgiveness of sins through Baptism, some allowed for a renewal of sorrow for later sins, others did not. Some churches followed the strict teaching suggested by St Paul in his Letter to the Romans (6:1-2) that Baptism was a cleansing that made a person dead to sin forever. Others looked more to the lenient texts such as Jesus' own insistence to Peter that sins should be forgiven past numbering (Mt 18:21-22). Other texts also suggested ways in which there should be a brotherly correction within the community. But there are no liturgies recorded for the forgiveness of sins.

This diversity within the Church began to decline with the adoption of Christianity as the official religion of the Roman Empire. There was a tendency to uniform the feasts and liturgies of the Church, centralising it on Rome itself with the strengthening of the authority of the pope and the licensing of 'Roman' texts for use throughout the Church. At this time, those who offended against the community or its members were put outside a sense of full communion. They remained Christians but became members of the Order of Penitents, who were known publicly as those who had offended and who were undergoing a period of reparation. That period could be long with severe penalties being inflicted. The system became unwieldy and impractical, and gradually ceased to exist.

Then from an unlikely source there came dramatic changes which were to have increasing influence for about three centuries and whose impact has never been lost in the understanding of the idea of God's forgiveness. The influence arose in the Celtic Church, in Ireland. The Irish Church had been isolated from Europe and Rome after the fall of the Roman Empire at the beginning of the fifth century. It had continued to grow around monasteries, so much so that the whole of the Celtic Church centred around monastic communities in the absence, perhaps, of any large towns. The monastic structure was less formal than would be familiar today, and monks pursued a spiritual companionship rather than the observance of a written rule. Young monks would gather as disciples of older and wiser men. As part of their spiritual formation, individuals would confess their sins and, along with an absolution, they would be given a penance, often quite rigorous and demanding. The hallmarks of this penitential system were that it allowed for failure and the admission of failure with the community and the ability to be forgiven through the performance of prayer and penance. It also allowed for a sense of 'learning from mistakes' and the ability to begin again. It encouraged a private forum in which faults could be admitted without a necessary sense of public disgrace.

The monastic penitential system grew in popularity. Tariffs of penances for various offences were listed in books called Penitentials so that some sort of uniformity was established. The use of the Penitentials gradually spread throughout the British Isles and into Northern Europe. Copies of the most famous Penitential Books were to be found in the great monasteries of Spain and Italy. They also went beyond the monastery walls to be used among those who had received formal education, the wealthier classes. It is not clear when this practice declined nor to what extent it was accepted in many places, but it is clear that its impact was enormous and widespread for a time.

It was not until about the twelfth century that a structure of the Sacrament of Reconciliation was fixed in a way that would be recognisable to us. This was something of a Golden Age for the Church when Christianity had established itself in a Europe which was more politically settled and which was beginning to flourish in the arts and sciences.

At this time a particularly important philosophical

dispute arose about the nature of forgiveness and how it was validly received in the sacramental forum. There were those who were known as 'contritionists' who believed that the validity of the sacrament was achieved through the sorrow, or contrition, shown and felt by the penitent, and that there could be no absolution from sin without suitable contrition. The 'absolutionists', on the other hand, believed that the power of the sacrament rested in the words of absolution and that forgiveness was validly conveyed by absolution whether the penitent felt contrition or not.

This philosophical argument was typical of the scholasticism of the time which manifested a desire to contain everything in a consistent, logical argument. However, the dilemma faced by the philosophers of the twelfth century is not lost on us. The absolutionists and the contritionists still exist in our day, and it is well to notice where the roots of modern understanding of the sacrament may lie. For there are those who have abandoned the use of the sacrament, reasoning that their sorrow, expressed in prayer, is sufficient for forgiveness. There are certainly many others who attend the sacrament because they do not believe that they can be forgiven without the words of absolution, spoken by the priest.

Tragically it was the abuses of the sacrament which so much concerned the Reformers. In an age which was preoccupied by death and judgement, the sacrament which conferred absolution was all too often used unscrupulously and its confidentiality breached. The sale of indulgences and absolution fired the cause of the Reformation and placed a burden of responsibility on the Church to give serious attention to these things, among other aspects of Church life and practice.

The Council of Trent confronted the abuses, and settled a form for the sacrament which was to remain virtually unchanged for almost three hundred years. The place for the sacrament was to be the confessional box, and the elements required for a valid celebration were the confession of sins, with contrition, and the receiving of penance and absolution. A renewed emphasis was placed on the confidentiality of the sacrament, and on the seal of the confession which utterly forbade the communication by the priest of anything said in the confession to a third person, on pain of excommunication. The legislation for this sacrament lent itself to the provision of formula prayers and a mechanical use of the confessional. While for a long time available only to adults, its use was extended to children when they were also invited to receive communion at a very early age.

Following the Second Vatican Council and its professed intention that all sacramental liturgies should be revised, the Sacrament of Reconciliation was the first to be renewed. Whilst still requiring that there should be the option for anonymity, a new emphasis was placed on a sense of freedom in a celebration between priest and penitent. It would be unfair to judge the quality of these reforms, since their implementation has not been widespread and they came at a time when the number of people using the confessional has diminished. Part 2 of this book will consider the new Rite, its strengths and innovations.

Chapter 3

The forgiving God

The way in which we approach the Sacrament of Reconciliation or indeed any sacrament will largely depend on the
notion that we have of the God in whom we believe. That
idea needs to grow and mature as we become more capable
of accepting the subtleties and sophistication of all that God
has revealed of himself and of his plan for salvation.

I wonder how often we stick rigidly to a primitive
notion of God and, because we give so little time to our
development of this image, it takes root and becomes quite
unassailable.

The image that we first have of God, in our childhood,
may well be shrouded in a sense of wonder, but it is also
surely identified very closely with parental authority, restrictions and not a little fear. 'Don't do that, it's naughty
and God will punish you.' Inevitably, at that early age, the
image of God is one of remoteness. No matter how hard a
child might be encouraged to talk to God and to believe
that God loves us all, God remains remote because he
cannot be seen or hugged and the places most associated
with him, the churches, are big and impersonal and full of
rules and regulations of liturgy. Most of us can probably
remember that it was the one hour of the week when we
had to be quiet, and be unnatural in our behaviour.

It must be an important part of the Christian pilgrimage
to grow in a vision of God. We cannot allow ourselves to
get rooted in a superficial view, but we must learn more
and more about God from the way that he has revealed
himself to us. We must return to the Scriptures, and to
Christ, in order to learn more of our God.

And so we must ask the question: who is God and what do we know of him? Even in his own self-revelation, he only gradually developed an image of himself in the understanding of his chosen people. God revealed himself to his people over the centuries only as fast as they were able to understand and accept. The God of Israel in the Old Testament is not a figure who is suddenly fully understandable; he remains swathed in mystery but, little by little, the people come to know him through the way he guides them and the way in which he speaks through the events of their history and the mouths of his prophets.

So it is that the God who first speaks to his people does so from a cloud, or from a mountain or a burning bush. He is remote, known only by his voice and his command. The first relationship of God with his people is one of king to subject. God is distant, powerful and demanding. In return for their obedience, he is protective and generous. It was only much later that the image of God was softened in the character of the shepherd, the vine-dresser, the lover of his people.

The whole of the Old Testament is a history of the chosen people, and it is more. The history not only records the past; but it also is one which constantly looks forward to the coming of the Messiah and the fulfilling of the promises that God had made, particularly in the prophecies of Isaiah, Jeremiah and Ezekiel.

But it is only in the coming of the Messiah that we see the fullest revelation of God and it is to Christ himself that we must turn if we are to see our God. It is Jesus, who is the perfect image of God, who shows us the qualities of God, expressed in a human form, '...to have seen me is to have seen the Father.' If we look carefully at everything that Christ reveals to us of his Father, we may well be pleasantly surprised. Jesus makes it very clear that he was sent by his Father for the weak, the sick and the sinners (Lk 5:31-32). There is no question that he had only come for those who were fit and intelligent, the superior classes of society. His ministry was spent among the poor; not only those who were materially poor, but the spiritually poor also. This confounded the Pharisees, who thought that the Messiah would want to eat with them and pray and teach among them and they questioned, with disdain, his habits of eating with the poor and the social outcasts, like the tax-collectors (Lk 5:30). The very fact that he did not spend his time in their company, except to argue with them and to point out their hypocrisy, was a source first for their jealousy and later for their determination to have him put to death (Lk 6:11). For the sinners, the poor and the outcast, however, all that Jesus said was utterly welcome. With the exception of the preaching of John the Baptist, it was the first time in generations that they were invited to believe that their situation was not hopeless. The established teachers of the law, the so-called 'righteous' men, the Pharisees, had offered nothing in the way of hope to those who had been born into poverty, or with physical disability or those who, through human weakness, had failed to live the law and the commandments.

In terms of the Jewish tradition, the poor were only poor because they had not found favour in God's eyes by their way of life. God directly rewarded goodness with a material well-being, it was thought. Therefore the poor were in their wretched condition simply because their lives deserved no better reward. In the same way, the crippled and the blind were disabled only because that was the consequence of either their own sins or the sins of their ancestors. That the Messiah should openly proclaim that he had not come for the righteous but for sinners gave them that hope which had so long been denied (Lk 5:32). And it must have been this teaching that made the crowds desperate to find Jesus and listen to all that he had to say (Lk 14:25).

We far too easily forget this fundamental attitude of Christ. As the Messiah, he knew that he was coming into a broken and sinful world and he was not coming merely to gather the righteous, those who had managed to cling to the truth and the law. He was always aware that his work must first of all be a mission of conversion, calling everyone to repentance. He told his disciples that their mission was to be to the whole world where there was a rich harvest waiting to be gathered in (Mt 28:19). All through the three years of his ministry, we find Christ teaching and going to the help of the very people whom society, and the so-called 'righteous' people, had rejected.

There was a sense of urgency in his work; everyone must be saved and all must be brought home to safety. The gospels make this very clear. When Jesus uses the Parable of the Lost Sheep (Lk 15:4-7) he is emphasising the insistence that all should be saved. And therefore the shepherd cannot allow one of the sheep to be lost, even though ninety-nine are safe. And notice, too, that when the shepherd finds the lost sheep, there is no punishment because it had gone astray. Quite the contrary, the shepherd rejoices because he was anxious about losing even one.

That same urgency is found in the priestly prayer of Jesus in the Gospel of John where he proclaims that his Father wants no-one to be lost, but that everyone should enjoy the salvation he has prepared for them (Jn 17:12).

Within his teaching we find the element of forgiveness constantly coming to the fore. Jesus was preceded by John whose message had been fundamentally one of repentance: 'Repent, for the kingdom of heaven is at hand' (Mt 3:2). John had begun the work that Jesus was to continue. He told the crowds that there was someone coming who was far greater than he could ever be and that he was not worthy even to undo the strap of his sandals (Mt 3:11). Jesus – the one for whom John was waiting and to whom he directed all the crowds who came to him – comes with the same message of repentance, that sins may be forgiven.

This attitude to forgiveness which shines through the whole of Jesus' ministry can well be described as lavish. It reaches in all directions, touching all types of people in every sort of circumstance. It was never refused. We need to call to mind only a few of the incidents of his ministry to see the generosity of Jesus that went to great lengths to express itself in forgiveness.

Jesus intended that forgiveness should be unlimited, and unconditional. The law of the Old Testament had called on the Jews to forgive seven times. This in itself was generous and marked a radical departure from the codes of law of the neighbouring nations. For most traditions of that time, the sense of retribution did not merely require doing to the criminal what he had done to his victim, but going much further so as to deter others. The notion of only 'an eye for an eye...' was already quite a development and the question of forgiving repeatedly was quite a unique notion. In effect it called on people to be prepared always to forgive. Peter had come to Jesus and reminded him of this precept of the Jewish law, and was probably pleased with himself for recognising the importance that Jesus attached to forgiveness. He must have been very surprised by Jesus' reply that seven times would not be enough; if required we must be prepared to forgive seventy times seven times, infinitely (Mt 18:21-22).

The Jewish law had been generous in demanding seven times. The use of the word seven is symbolic, standing as the perfect number and meaning a sense of completeness. Even in the law, then, there was to be no lack of willingness to forgive. Jesus extends this to a figure which is almost beyond calculation, so great is his desire to see forgiveness manifested.

Forgiveness was not just something that Jesus demanded of others. Throughout his ministry, Jesus himself forgave without hesitation. It was precisely in that moment when we might have expected him finally to be judgemental that he showed the true depth of his desire to forgive. During the excruciating agony of the crucifixion Jesus forgave twice: first those who were in the act of putting him to death (Lk 23:33-34) and then the thief who was being crucified with him; a man who admitted his crime and accepted that this was the punishment for what he had done (Lk 23:39-43).

On the occasions where Jesus performed miraculous cures, he often forgave the individuals before curing them, the physical cure being a proof to the crowds that he had the power to forgive sins. This is clearly shown in the episode where a man is let down through the roof in order to get access to Jesus since the crowds were so great. The man had been brought before Jesus in order that he could be healed, but Jesus forgives him his sins first of all, before performing the cure, to show the priority of forgiveness (Lk 5:18-25). This incident is important for another reason. It shows Jesus forgiving someone because of the faith of others. We are not told what the man himself believed, nor whether he was hoping for a miracle to remove his paralysis. What we are told is that Jesus forgave the man his sins because he saw the faith of those who had carried him to the place and let him down through the roof.

Jesus was eager to forgive even when that forgiveness was not sought. He forgave those who put him to death. He forgave the woman who had been found committing adultery when the Pharisees wanted to stone her. She asked for nothing but received a reprieve from the punishment and forgiveness.

Jesus never turned anybody away. Whoever sought his forgiveness received it. There were no exceptions and no conditions attached, other than the invitation to go and sin no more.

It is important, too, to see the close connection that Jesus made between forgiveness and love. Sin burdens our lives, but its effects may be cancelled out by the good that may be achieved through love which is shown. A woman who was known to be a prostitute came to Jesus and washed his feet with her tears, anointing them with perfumed oil. Jesus' reasoning is simple: 'I tell you, her sins, which are many, are forgiven, for she loved much; but he who is forgiven little, loves little' (Lk 7:37-38,47-50).

We would be foolish to conclude our use of the Scriptures without remembering that there are many other passages which are judgemental and castigating. Jesus often makes statements which seem to indicate that we can never be worthy of eternal life; we are doomed to be rejected by God because we will never be able to reach the standards which so much of the Gospel requires. But we must see the passages in their own context. When Jesus is angry and judgemental he is speaking to crowds who are being self-righteous. His criticism is against any feelings of complacency. He constantly warns the Pharisees and the Sadducees of the doom that awaits them because they have blinded themselves and condemned themselves by their own arrogance.

It is in fact a sign of Christ's true love for all that leads him to be so critical of these people – he loves them enough to want to open their eyes to their own mistakes. We may use the analogy of a parent's love for a child. Sometimes love must be expressed in a rebuke, in discipline and firmness. 'Don't run across the busy road, because it's dangerous'; 'Don't go near the fire, you will hurt yourself'. There are so many times when a parent must say 'don't' but only because it is for the child's good. Jesus needed to speak strongly to some of those who came to listen to him, and to argue with him, because they were in very grave danger of reaping the rewards of their own stupidity and arrogance.

But for those who acknowledged their need and their own faults and failings, there was only ever a welcome of compassion and encouragement.

Probably none of the passages that we have referred to from Scripture will have been new to you. The trouble is that they are possibly all too familiar and we have ceased to read them and reflect on them. Our God is, first and foremost, a God of love. He loves us so much that he sent his Son who could be the clearest possible picture of himself and who, by his death and resurrection, could establish our redemption.

This God of ours is persistent. He refuses to stop loving us and, when we fall away from the right road, he is insistent on seeking us out and bringing us home. No-one is excluded from this love and it is those who seem to be in the most need that he is most eager to find. Weak or strong, his invitation is open to all, for Christ's final command to his disciples was to go out to the whole world (Mt 28:19). We know that he welcomes the return of those whose actions have taken them a long way from goodness for Jesus forgave the adulteress, the prostitute, the thief and the tax-collector. For those who understand their need for forgiveness, there is nothing more than words of encouragement.

We must never allow ourselves to think that it may be all very well for God to forgive all these individuals but that, of course, he does not know me or my sins. There is a tendency to exclude ourselves because we do not believe that God could be that interested in me, or that he would continue to forgive someone who is so persistently failing to live the Christian life. The answer to this myth is to be found throughout the Scriptures. To Jeremiah, the prophet who thought himself incapable of such a role, God said: 'Before I formed you in the womb I knew you, and before you were born I consecrated you' (Jer 1:5). The psalmist also makes it clear that there is nothing in our lives of which God is not fully aware:

O Lord, you search me and you know me,
you know my resting and my rising,
you discern my purpose from afar.
You mark when I walk or lie down,
all my ways lie open to you.

(Ps 139)

The full quality of God's loving forgiveness is seen in the remarkable text of the Parable of the Prodigal Son (Lk 15:11-32). We will be considering that passage later. The text has been reproduced in full in Appendix I because it is so rich in the explanation of God's desire to forgive. In no other passage in the Scriptures do we glimpse such a quality of reconciliation, where forgiveness brings no con-demnation but a reinstatement of dignity and self-respect, with words of encouragement.

It is in the light of this image of God that we must

consider the Sacrament of Reconciliation. Clearly, just as we need to take this view of God with us in our reflection on the sacrament, so we must leave misconceptions behind. There are so many myths in our thinking about God, and many of them are, no doubt, subconscious. We must be sure to root out any ideas that God is a bully, or an angry parent or a cold-blooded hanging judge who demands perfection. Our God is patient and infinitely understanding. He knows all our weaknesses and difficulties and is hardly surprised when, despite our efforts, we fall into the same faults repeatedly.

This sacrament is a means by which we can have restored to us something of the love that God first lavished upon us in creation. It is a means towards the end of being united with God. If our image of God includes a trust in the fact that he really is longing to forgive, then we can see that this sacrament is immensely important. In each of the sacraments God touches our lives with his power, and so the fulness of the sacrament is the joining of our own contribution with God's gift. God's role in the celebration of this sacrament is consistent, but the value that we may receive from it will vary according to our understanding of it and our preparation for its celebration. We have completed a first step in our attempts to understand the design of God in the sacrament. Now we must turn our minds to the human element.

Chapter 4

Obstacles to the celebration of the sacrament

The celebration of the Sacrament of Reconciliation has suffered through the addition of a clutter of elements of human origin, and in each individual celebration a long list of obstacles exists which may detract from its value and its success. As we shall see, the celebration of the sacrament requires very few elements; it is an occasion of great freedom. But its freedom also makes it vulnerable. So very little is required for its technical validity but so much depends on the contribution made both by the priest and the penitent. If the sacrament were to rely more on a planned presentation, a formal liturgy with set prayers and readings, with all the content very carefully defined, then its celebration would, in that sense, be relatively simple and straightforward.

However, this sacrament is far more ambitious. It must be wide enough to embrace the experience of human life. It must offer a place in which not just the mundane and familiar may be expressed, but also the rare and sometimes unique joys and dilemmas of the Christian who is striving (and so often failing) to live the Christian life of the Gospel.

When we speak of the 'obstacles' to celebrating this sacrament, we are speaking of those elements, some of them material, some psychological, which deprive the penitent of the freedom which is intended in the sacrament. Some concern the time, the place and the forum in which the sacrament is celebrated; others will touch on the language used, and others still will be directly connected with the education, the experience and the expectation of the penitent. Much, too, will depend on the attitude and the skill of the priest and on his own expectation and experience which he will draw from his roles, both as minister of the sacrament and also as the penitent when he, too, avails himself of the sacrament.

There is no possibility that we could identify all the obstacles, let alone remove them. But we may set ourselves the more modest and attainable tasks of considering a few of the more obvious ones and some ways in which these difficulties may be resolved or at least reduced. Any further progress must then be left to the individual to make a personal assessment of their own attitude to the sacrament; identifying what is different and why; what sort of clutter interferes with it and how it may be removed.

The language

Even the language which surrounds the Sacrament of Reconciliation is a major obstacle for some people. The traditional word 'confession' conjures up negative feelings. We seem now to have lost, through the course of time and the development of language, any positive meaning to the word confession. In its mediaeval use the title 'Confessor' was indeed one of the highest compliments which could be paid, and confessors ranked as a distinguished class among those who were proclaimed and canonised saints of the Church. The title of 'Confessor' was bestowed on the Saxon King of England, St Edward, because in his reign he so consistently promoted and practised the truths of the Gospel. He 'confessed' his faith by announcing it and witnessing to it. This sense of dignity and, indeed, virtue which was once attached to the word has now disappeared and we are left with a negative and demeaning sense.

We would tend to think of something which is confessed as being awful; the admission of which carries a sense of shame and degradation. We use the word in association with the image of a criminal who, having been found out, breaks down and confesses his crime. Where someone confesses, there is an implication that he is now at the mercy of someone else; there is no room for negotiation; there can only be an appeal for mercy. In our modern sense, the one who confesses does so because of pressure from others. It represents a final collapse in which dignity is lost.

Something of this association with the meaning of the word must colour our attitude to a sacrament which is called 'confession'. Even though we are now encouraged to call it the Sacrament of Reconciliation, this new title does not seem to have been whole-heartedly accepted. Somehow the title in the parish newsletter of 'Times of Confession' and our own familiar use of the phrase 'going to confession' do not easily give way to the more technical phraseology of the Sacrament of Reconciliation and Reconciliation Rooms.

It is doubtful that we will succeed in supplanting the word confession with anything else. Language has its own way of developing and phrases which have become so familiar cannot simply be uprooted and replaced by design. But just as words such as 'awful' and 'terrific' are now accepted as carrying meanings which are quite remote from the meanings that they originally had, so other words such as 'confession' and 'martyr' must be allowed to retain in religious terms meanings which have changed in their secular context.

Moving on from the awkwardness of the word 'confession' and the feelings with which it may be associated, we have a major obstacle concerning the language which is used in the celebration of the sacrament. Something of this was mentioned in Chapter 1 where it was seen that confessions are often shrouded in generalities. The mistake which seems to have been made is that an artificial and private language has come to be used here which is employed nowhere else. The consequence is that when I come to confession, I have to translate the reality of my life into the accepted language of the confessional. This might have been acceptable but for the fact that, since we learned the language at such an early age, the vocabulary that we use is very limited. It is by no means unusual that, the confession having been made, the penitent continues by saying, 'Can I ask you something, Father?' or 'I have a problem that I want to discuss.' It is only then that there is a possibility to step outside the confessional language and begin to talk about life as it is. Surely, it should be life itself which is the subject of what is spoken in the confessional!

There is a further consequence of the problem that we have already mentioned: that most of us learn the fundamental practice of the sacrament when we are very young and the practice does not mature in relation to the demands of our lives. The language that we use must extend and become more sophisticated if it is to express the complexities of our adult life. In truth, there should be no 'language of the confessional'. All the stock phrases by which we were first introduced to the sacrament, such as 'I have told lies, I have been disobedient', should be shaken off with those childhood disciplines which, while so important in their place and providing such fundamental education, become redundant because life becomes more sophisticated and mature.

The importance of language must not be underestimated in this sacrament for, in many respects and in most instances, it will provide the key to the good use of the sacrament. Of course there are times when precision in language is hard because it is so difficult to express emotions and feelings, and there is often a confusion about life and its problems which cannot be put into words but only expressed in generalities. For the most part, though, we will draw much more from this sacrament if we can approach it with precision. There is a most important element in the sacrament which is self-understanding. The better I know myself and the more clearly I see my mistakes, the more positively I can draw from the sacrament and benefit by it.

The time and place

Everybody is susceptible to atmosphere and the circumstances in which something takes place. Just as it is very difficult to have an important and soul-searching conversation when there is loud music and people are crowding round, so it is very difficult to be festive and to host other people having just heard some personally sad or tragic news. Both can be done but only when there is a considerable effort of will-power, in that first instance, to block other people and noise out and not be distracted from the conversation at hand, in the second instance by blocking or overcoming the sense of sadness and grief in order to put on the vivaciousness of a good host.

The same sort of criteria apply to our celebration of the sacrament. We can, of course, overcome certain difficulties by determination and concentration, but how much easier it is to celebrate reconciliation in an atmosphere which suits the occasion. We will all differ in our preferences but there are certain guidelines which should be obvious, and are worth promoting.

It may well be quite appropriate for priests to hear confessions in the fields surrounding Lourdes, Medjugorje and other places of pilgrimage because the atmosphere of the place does not detract from the celebration. But the hearing of a confession in the nave of a busy cathedral full of tourists, or in the porch of a parish church, is bound to be an obstacle either to the penitent or to the quality of his or her confession. Similarly as regards the need for sound-proofing of the place in which the confession is being heard. There are confessional rooms in parishes which are used for the storage of books and furniture when they should be places given over worthily to the celebration of a sacrament. There are many confessional boxes which are dark and dirty.

Time is also very important when considering the obstacles to the celebration of the sacrament. The problem of time will be almost impossible to resolve. There are some confessions which will require only two or three minutes. But there are others which require much more time if the penitent is to be properly accommodated. Most confessions would fall between these two extremes but, within any given group of people on any particular day, it will be impossible to judge what length of time will be required. Further, there are all the frustrations and exasperations when a priest or penitent requires time to speak but one or both are aware that others are waiting.

Scruples

Among the most unpleasant elements which appear in confession are scruples. They come in all sorts of degrees; there is probably a trace of scruple in most confessions, and they are dangerous not only because they depress the penitent but because they undermine a realistic and constructive view of God and hamper a person's efforts to live the Christian faith.

In their worst form, scruples manifest themselves as a crippling insecurity and a belief that any confession that is made is inadequate. Those people with severe scruples see no possibility of being at peace with God, and think that nothing in their lives is ever free from sin. For some people there is the dread that every action is undertaken for the wrong motive and in their opinion it would have been better had they not begun the action. No matter how much they may hate their sins, they feel that they cannot help but commit them, and that they must carry the burden of guilt for having done so, a guilt which is never really taken away even by sacramental absolution. Scruples so root themselves in people that eventually every thought and action becomes riddled with feelings of guilt and every day is spent worrying about all that could possibly have gone wrong.

But scrupulosity seems to appear in a mild form in the confession of most people, whether it be in the belief that a person is guilty of something even though they did not consent to what had happened (like missing Mass because of a broken leg), or in being incapable of letting go of the guilt for sins once committed and now forgiven. Scruples would seem to arise simply through an ignorance of what the Sacrament of Reconciliation does, and a failure to reflect on the quality of the forgiveness of God.

The beginnings of scruples could lie within any number of circumstances. The child who is constantly told that his or her efforts are not good enough, or of whom more is constantly demanded, translates the image of a demanding parent into the image of God. The child who is always reminded of past disobedience to parents will find in his or her image of God the list of sins that remain forever, which God intends to punish. The genuinely religious person, beginning to understand the full scope of Christianity and its invitation to perfection, becomes overwhelmed by the failure to attain the desired standards in life and prayer. In my experience this has happened to individuals who suddenly have recovered a desire to take their faith seriously after a period away from its practice, and also in those who have chosen to be received into the Church. In both these cases there seems to be the possibility that the personal desire to become perfect in living the Gospel far outstrips the actual performance; 'I cannot be as good as I want and need to be.' A sense of scrupulosity is born through the frustration of judging oneself to be a failure. The most numerous group of scrupulous people are those who disappoint or shock themselves by a particular incident or sin in life and may feel that it can never be forgiven. Then life becomes a daily failing struggle against guilt.

And it is hardly fair to level this against religion. It seems, on the contrary, to be part of a much more common experience of humanity. Everybody makes mistakes and does things wrong. There is a sense of right and wrong in each of us – call it conscience or not – which may be highly offended by something that we do. It will register a sense of embarrassment at best, or at worst a feeling of shock and

51

deep-rooted guilt. Whether we are religious people or not, we will all remain victim to the memory of whatever it is that makes us feel guilty and uncomfortable. But for those who are scrupulous and who labour under a harsh and unforgiving image of God, that discomfort can nag to the point that whatever went wrong has now become the unmovable and unforgivable barrier between them and God.

In all these cases, God is imagined as someone who is judgemental, remote and frightening. He is sensed as a God who has no warmth or love, who teases us by inviting all to eternal life and who then makes it impossible for all but the very few to receive such life. He is seen to be a God who delights in the legal technicalities of perfect confession and contrition, prepared to annul his absolution for sins whenever there is even the slightest hesitation or imperfection on our part.

But this is not our God. He has not revealed himself to us in this way and we have no right to imagine or proclaim him as such. Christ is the image of God and all that we see of him in the gospels is full of compassion and forgiveness. He urges and encourages us to begin again when things have gone wrong – and we must not see God as insisting on anything else.

How can we be sure that God is so keen to forgive? Could it be that all this talk is just wishful thinking? Where is the proof? We have only to look at the gospels and the life of Christ to see that forgiveness and mercy are to be found everywhere, and there is no limit to the encouragement of Christ for those who fall short of perfection. It is certainly true that Christ also expresses anger against the Scribes and the Pharisees, but this was because they were the teachers and leaders and had laid heavy burdens upon their people. Christ rebuked them because they refused to encourage the people; because they insisted on the fulfilment of the law, for its own sake.

A further proof that God longs to forgive is seen in the sacraments that Christ gave to his Church. Of those seven sacraments, no less that four include forgiveness. In Baptism, the original sin of mankind is washed away so that we may be free to pursue goodness in our lives. In the Anointing of the Sick, forgiveness is bestowed on the sick or the dying in anticipation of their return to the Lord so that they may come to him freed from all their sins. The forgiveness is freely bestowed even when a person is too ill at that moment to request it. In the Eucharist we celebrate the new and everlasting covenant when Christ redeemed us from our sins by his sacrifice on the cross. If all this were not enough Christ, through the Church, brings a sacrament which is entirely dedicated to forgiveness – the Sacrament of Reconciliation. Such a lavish display cannot leave us in doubt that God longs to forgive. We have no right and no evidence to doubt that.

Some people find apparent evidence for their fear of judgement in the Books of the Old Testament, but in this we must progress very carefully, because the Old Testament is not easy, and needs an expert interpretation.

It could be said that we all have some sense of scruples in our lives, and we must be firm in recognising them for what they are. If they are there, then there is every likelihood that they will grow and become a worry. So our attitude to them must be determined from the beginning.

The cure for scruples would simply be to recognise and deeply accept two truths. The first is that God is Love, perfect Love. Part of his love must necessarily be that he longs to forgive us for all that separates us from him. The second is that we are all sinners – every one of us falling far short of the perfection to which we are all invited by Christ. But despite our failure, God's love for us remains constant.

Having identified our failings, or at least some of them, we place them before God and ask for forgiveness. In forgiving, God takes all the guilt and the burden of the past away from us; he does not want us to be weighed down by it all any longer. The invitation is to begin again, recognising where we go wrong but not worrying about it. Our main concern is, and must be, to concentrate on doing what is right, bringing love and compassion to those whom God places in our lives each day – they are our neighbours, placed in our day by God because he wants us to give his love to them. It is not by chance that they are there. God's plan for us is complete in every detail and people come into our lives because there is some reason for them to be there. It frustrates our mission as Christians if we spend our lives worrying about what has or might have gone wrong, rather than in seeking to do now what is right.

Chapter 5

Making better use of the sacrament

How do we make better use of confession? There must, first of all, be adequate preparation. So much of what may be achieved is not available if a person simply turns up at confession, or happens to see that there is a priest hearing confessions and there is no queue. In order to enter into the proper context of the sacrament I must ask myself about my relationship with God, with my family and the community in which I live and work. What sort of things have I done which are wrong and for which I must accept responsibility? They may be things to do with my spiritual life, my relationships, my own dignity. I must be prepared to ask whether there are specific things which have occurred where I have not behaved in a Christ-like way; things which were lacking in love and offended my God-given dignity. I will not remember everything that has gone wrong, but that does not matter. The more important offences against God will show themselves to me in my reflections because they will be the ones which are more obviously 'on my conscience'. In Chapters 8 and 9 in Part 2, some more detailed explanation is giving as to how this self-searching may be put into practice.

There is another side to our preparation which is often apparently entirely forgotten. It is not so much concerned with what I have done which was wrong, but rather what I have failed to do which would be right. This was commonly known in the past as the sin of omission, though not many people would use that title now. However, it forms a most important part of what we are, and it needs to be carefully considered.

Jesus most certainly condemned what was wrong and warned his followers away from what should not be done. He was very direct in his condemnation of hypocrisy, and spoke out against greed and selfishness. But the greater part of what he had to teach concerned what his followers should be seeking to do. In his ministry, Jesus taught, by word and action, the way of love. He showed us that loving other people was full of hard work, requiring generosity and selflessness. He exhausted himself when he was with the crowds because he responded to their needs. Even when exhausted with teaching, he still made time for who-ever needed his help. He even went without sleep and food because there was no time – the crowds demanded his attention. If anyone had the right to tailor his own ministry, it was Jesus. As the Messiah, God's only Son, we might have expected him to have come in quite a different way. The Jews expected a princely Messiah who would free them from the occupation and domination of the Romans and who would make Israel a politically great nation again, as it had been under King Solomon. Or indeed, Jesus might have chosen to be a teacher moving in the intellectual circles that were well established in Jerusalem. But he allowed his work to be dictated to him by the needs of those who came to him and who asked him for help. Quite astonishingly the work of Jesus was decreed by the needs of the poor, the sick and the spiritually needy.

It was by the very fact that he entered so completely into the human condition that Jesus was able to become a complete model for us. He lived what he taught and his life was full of all the incidents and experiences which are common to us all. It was this combination of teaching immersed into life that was his ministry. To want to be a follower of Christ means to accept the invitation to undertake that same ministry – for it is that ministry which Jesus con-ferred upon his apostles which has, in turn, been handed on to us. Our lives and actions must be interpreted in the light of that mission which has been undertaken. Equally, it should be our confession which reflects not only an awareness of our failure by doing things that are wrong, but also our failure to take the opportunity to do something more of what is right. Indeed, we need to bear in mind that we are not only disciples of Christ but also called on by him to be 'other Christs' to the world and to carry on all that he had begun in communicating God's Word.

That sort of commission requires that we be creative and grasp the opportunities to do something out of love, just as Jesus allowed all that he did to be the consequence of that invitation to love. When we fail to reflect this ministry, we should want to be able to recognise the fault and to ask for forgiveness. This belongs to our preparation for the sacrament, too.

One of the greatest challenges that we face daily as followers of Christ is precisely the task of deciding how best we can fulfil his command to love in the circumstances of our lives. It is not always obvious what we should do, and there are decisions to be made every day. The examples could be endless. Perhaps we see someone who is upset and we ask ourselves how best we might show love to that person. We must make our own judgement, which is based on what we know about the person and the incident which may have upset them. In some cases we will judge that love demands that we speak to them and try to offer comfort by being with them. But sometimes it may be better to leave them alone, because they need time to themselves. But we may be sure that our concern at all times to try to be loving will help us to come to the best decision. If we discover that we have made the wrong choice, then we may learn from the mistake and be a little wiser about people and their needs. There will be decisions to be made in all our tasks and in the time we spend with other people, and in each decision there is the guiding principle of Christ's invitation to love.

The better we are in touch with ourselves and the sort of decisions that we are making in our lives, the more we are able to reflect on the type of people that we are, the easier will be the preparation for confession. I shall know what I am looking for and what the major difficulties are likely to be because I shall be aware of what has been wrong in the past. I shall be able to reflect on my decisions and my behaviour to discover where I have acted well and been able to see and respond to other people's needs. This is the ministry of Jesus himself, being reflected (however falteringly and incompletely) in my life. In this way, my life becomes guided by something far more challenging than just 'keeping the rules'. Because I am trying to imitate the goodness and creative love of Jesus, I have the invitation to see everything that I do as an opportunity; and opportunities require reflection and deliberation. Being Christian really does require a lot of careful attention and hard work.

As I become more capable of looking at myself, I shall also learn to distinguish between the surface sin and its roots, and this will represent a very significant step forward both in the way that I understand myself and the benefit that I may obtain in the sacrament. For example, when someone says that they are often angry and impatient, it is important not just to confess the sins of anger and impatience but to recognise that there is probably something which makes that person react in that way – and it is the cause of the sin that needs the attention. After all, if you walk into a room at home and find the floor under two inches of water, it is no good simply mopping it up without finding the source and plugging the leak, for as often as you fill a bucket, as much, if not more, water will have taken its place. It may be necessary to tolerate the flooded floor until the source of the danger has been found and properly repaired, and only then will our attempts to get rid of all the water have some lasting effect.

So many of the things that we understand to be obviously wrong in our lives are secondary products of difficulties that are not so easily seen, but if we are to deal effectively with the secondary sins, we must find and cure the root problem, which is the cause. Someone who confesses to drinking too much might well discover that the real problem lies in his frustration with his job or a worrying problem in his home or marriage. By searching for the real cause and tackling the roots of the sin in such a case, the apparent surface sin – the excessive drinking – is quite likely to cease of its own accord. What was thought to be a problem in itself has proved itself to be the signal of other unhappiness, the alarm bell for something else which is wrong.

It is important, if I am to use the sacrament properly, that I bring myself and my own particular sins and obstacles to the confession. Using formulas of words which I learned years ago will not say anything about me or my current needs. It makes sense to tell the priest how long it is since the last confession, my approximate age and whether married or not. This will be most useful to the priest in helping him to understand what I have to say, and in assisting him should he want to say something in return. So often what is said by the penitent says nothing about them as individuals and can provide a screen which allows the priest no access, no way of offering help. Rather than repeating a familiar list, or trying to include every last detail, I should be looking for the two or three most important difficulties I am encountering – by my very appearance at the sacrament, I have already shown that I am sorry for all my faults and failings and it is understood that, by the words of absolution, all my sins will be forgiven. By indicating two or three things in particular, I highlight those areas of my life about which I am most concerned. This, surely, is a more creative way of approaching God for forgiveness and would help us to mature in our relationship with him.

In the Parable of the Prodigal Son, the father might well have required a full account of how the son had squandered the money and all that had happened. But the father asked for no explanation because the son had recognised his fundamental mistake – that he had offended against heaven and against his father and that he was no longer worthy to be called a son. The father simply wanted to forgive. It was enough for the father that the son had found the courage to return home so that he could be forgiven.

So it is with God. He does not require endless details. He is well aware of what has happened. He surely prefers constructive consideration of the more important things which not only need forgiveness but which also need his help. The Sacrament of Reconciliation is part of the Christian pilgrimage. We should emerge from it not only forgiven but reconciled and strengthened. We need also to be confident about all that we have achieved in the sacrament, and the completeness of the forgiveness that God has bestowed.

Chapter 6

The priest and the sacrament

The role of the priest in the Sacrament of Reconciliation must not be overlooked. It is an essential role and one which can so easily be taken for granted, both by priest and penitent. It would be my contention that it is a role that has long been undervalued, not least by the priest but also by those responsible for the training of priests.

My own experience is probably not untypical. Within the seven years spent in training for the priesthood, I can only recall two pastoral sessions dedicated to the subject of this sacrament, one of which included a role play with fellow students. It would seem to me to be essential that this part of the priests' ministry be given a good deal of attention because it is not something that is predictable. We have seen in the preceding pages that there is an enormous freedom within the sacrament, allowing for an independent expression which is not to be found in the other sacraments, and this freedom must be welcomed by the priest and met with a competency.

Confession is not a place for solving problems. There may be questions that can and should be answered by the priest and there may be advice that can be given, but the central role of the priest in confession is not to answer or to advise; it is to stand as a mediator between God and the individual and to convey God's forgiveness for sins.

Taking this as the foundation point of priestly service in this context, there is indeed much that can be said about what the priest should intend to do and what he might be able to bring to each individual confession. There are skills and gifts which the priest may well use to enhance his role,

61

but the original foundation point must not be lost. Whenever a priest acts within his priestly ministry, he needs to be aware that he is taking part in something which is much greater than himself. The tasks that he performs are not things that he has undertaken for himself, but rather something to which he has been called within his vocation. We have made the mistake, too often, of identifying the man with the office, placing the priest on the pedestal and expecting a perfection of life and ministry from him which, when not duly delivered, results in a condemnation of both the priest and his efforts at ministry, and probably the Church as well.

But the priest is just an ordinary man who could no doubt have been engaged in one of any number of different occupations had he not felt that he had been called to serve God specifically within the ministry. And just like any ordinary person he has his own weaknesses and sinfulness, and he labours under much the same burdens of distraction, inconsistencies and failure. He, too, will have the need to receive absolution with the Sacrament of Reconciliation just as he gives it in God's name. Indeed, part of the strength that he can bring to the sacrament is that he has experienced many of the same trials and disappointments as those who come to him.

A priest can offer an incredible service to the penitent by providing essential ingredients to the sacrament. It is by no means my intention to list things, in a sort of recipe, which need to be mechanically inserted into each confession. Some elements will be helpful at one moment and inappropriate in the next. But I am convinced that the priest has a wealth of treasures by which he may enrich the celebration of the sacrament.

There is an opportunity, first and foremost, to introduce the fact of God's love. Do the penitents know that God loves them, as they are? Do they know that God has always loved them – even loved them into being – and that, as St Paul says, nothing can ever separate them from the love of Christ? This simple fact is often an eye-opener, particularly for someone who has come to the sacrament in fear. There seem to be so many people who regard the sacrament as the ticket by which they may avoid the anger and judgement of God. They have forgotten, or perhaps have never allowed themselves to grasp, the fact that God's love is there and does not need to be earned. So the very moment when they feel most distanced from God and of least value in God's eyes, and their own eyes too, is a particularly good moment to remind them that this is so. The reaction can sometimes be remarkable, and this can be the first step in prompting a re-evaluation of what has just been included in their confession, and of the sacrament itself. It may also be a trigger of release of the tensions and emotions which have made the penitent feel at rock-bottom. Imagine the woman, married with family growing up, who manages to overcome the obstacle that has distanced her from the Church for years, and confesses an abortion in the distant past. Or perhaps the professional married man, a leader of the local Church community, who confesses adultery; even though he readily and gladly admits that his marriage is happy. Such people have suffered much merely in the full recognition and realisation of what they have done. It has cost them even to come to the sacrament – their very being there may represent the end of a long struggle and a history of guilt – and these people need to be welcomed with the assurance that God loves them, always has done so, even in those dark moments when they have disappointed and even shocked themselves by what they have done.

There is no less a need to reassure others of God's love when they simply feel a little frustrated by their lack of progress, by habitual failings or by that notorious and universal sin – distraction in prayer. At such moments, should we not be much more concerned with the fact that they are there at all? This is the time to think of the father in the Parable of the Prodigal Son, running to meet the shamed younger son as he returns home, so that he could embrace him and welcome him back.

And if we are to reassure ourselves that God loves us,

then we must be clear that this love needs to be met with love and not fear. It is surely a nonsense to fear God. Think for a moment of someone that you love very much. How would you feel if that person came to you and said that although they knew very well that you loved them, they in return were very afraid of you? What a dreadful blow that would be, quite heart-breaking. But is not that what we are so often saying in our relationship with God? Yes, I know you love me, but I am afraid of you.

Deriving necessarily from that constant gift of God's love for each person, is his longing to forgive. It must surely be one of the essential qualities of love that it bears forgiveness. God is perfect Love and therefore he could not withhold forgiveness. It must always be available. That was the lesson that Jesus wanted Peter to learn when he insisted that to forgive seven times is not enough, but to be willing, indeed wishing, to forgive an incalculable number of times is what is required. This again may well come as a surprise to a penitent and be something that the priest may do well to introduce into the confession. Forgiveness is not something to be begged for, in God's eyes. Like the father in the parable he will, if given the opportunity, run to us as soon as he sees us approaching in order that forgiveness may be the more readily given.

For some people, it seems, this is an almost impossible reality to grasp; particularly for those people who seem to be dogged by habits that they cannot break, and by sins that seem to repeat themselves no matter how hard they may try to exclude them. This realisation of God's longing to forgive is difficult for us to accept because it seems so remote from our human experience. We know how hard it can be to forgive even once and harder still a second time. There soon comes a moment when, almost for our own protection, we have to say that enough is enough and to exclude a person from our life, because we feel that we have been hurt enough. Because this is our human experience, it is difficult to persuade ourselves that God does not behave in this way. It is important that the priest be able to remind us that God does not work in human ways. His patience is not limited and there is no moment when he finally cuts himself off, ending the covenant that he has with each one of us.

But there are important obligations that are born in the wake of God's overwhelming generosity. The Sacrament of Reconciliation is no slot-machine that merely produces an absolution, the whole event being isolated. The reality of God's love, expressed in this endless longing to forgive us, needs to be accepted with responsibility. If I am serious about celebrating that love of God for me and in receiving his forgiveness, then I need to be clear about the invitation that these bring: an invitation to begin again. It would be very callous, on our part, simply to accept love and forgiveness without wanting to respond.

It is for the priest to remind us that our response is vital and should contain three elements. In the first place, the response must be to accept the invitation to begin again – to be prepared to wipe the slate clean as a result of God's generosity and to make a new start. This in itself is difficult for many people. The formulas that are so often used in the confession include phrases which ask for forgiveness for all the sins of our past life, and in such phrases we see that so many people insist on hanging on to the past, dragging with them the burden of all that has gone wrong. While God may have forgiven them, they have not been able to forgive themselves. But the sacrament is intended to remove all the guilt of the past, so that we are free to make that new beginning.

The other two elements concern the way that we should approach that new beginning. We need to learn from the past and also to look for opportunities to do a little more of what is right and good. More about this was said in the preceding chapter when we considered the Sacrament of Reconciliation in the context of our lives, rather than as an event complete in itself.

In reminding penitents of these elements, the priest is assisting them in understanding the breadth of the sacrament, that it is part of a process and that its celebration brings consequences and challenges. Within this framework the priest may also do so much more. He may create a sense of welcome, perhaps defusing the nervousness and apprehension that a person feels. He may encourage them to say all that they want to say, and re-assure them that there is nothing so terrible that it should be hidden from God's forgiveness. He may also gently probe to clarify what has been said.

Concerning that, there are many difficulties that may arise and they should be well understood by both the priest and the penitent. There has been all too much sadness caused by misunderstanding. The law concerning the sacrament insists that a priest should not interrogate the penitent, but there is a possibility of probing a little to understand what has been said so as to clarify the situation. But this needs to be done with great sensitivity. A question may easily look like the beginning of an interrogation if it is not introduced gently. There are, however, ways in which a priest may introduce his questions so that he does not appear threatening.

It is important that the priest has the opportunity to seek further information because the clarification may so often be of benefit to the penitent, and indeed lead to the discovery that what has been confessed is not sinful at all. There have been those who thought certain days to be Days of Obligation when in fact they were not. As a consequence they worry about failing in their religious obligations when, indeed, no such obligations exist. Simple questions here can not only put someone's mind at rest, but also prove to be a source of education for them. This, of course, is just one of innumerable situations which may arise. The priest must judge when to pursue something that has been said – and to pursue it for the penitent's advantage – and balance that with the right to privacy which every individual enjoys within the confession.

This can, on the other hand, go badly wrong, perhaps all the more so when the confession takes place between a priest and penitent who are strangers to one another, in the anonymity of the confessional box. Here there is the danger of the misinterpretation of the tone of voice ('That priest sounded very unfriendly' or 'he just started asking questions') or there may be a genuine misunderstanding of what the penitent has just said. Both the priest and the penitent need to be patient about this and to seek the understanding that should be part of the good celebration of the sacrament. It is here, in fact, that formulas of words may have their value; they are immediately understood and recognisable. But all the dangers exist that nothing is expressed from the heart and an escape route is found to be available through the use of something familiar. If our preparation is good, it will bring a clarity to what we have to say.

Chapter 7

Meditation: Which son are you?

There are two sons in the Parable of the Prodigal Son. They play very different parts in the story which gives us a stunning insight into our God who has chosen to reveal himself as one who forgives and reconciles. The two roles depicted by the sons are not mutually exclusive, and we may find ourselves identifying with the characteristics of either or both. But whoever we are, perhaps we can learn something of ourselves and the overwhelming quality of the forgiveness of our God from this most powerful parable. (The text is given in Appendix I.)

The younger son is the familiar adolescent of any generation. He sees an excitement to life but always some-where else. The familiar surroundings of family and work are boring and irrelevant in the face of the excitement of other places, where real life is to be lived to the full. There is no understanding or appreciation of what he has: a home, family and security. Such things are taken for granted. This son is probably unaware of what his relationship is with his father; the awkward generation gap means that he feels frustrated and misunderstood. He does what most young people would only dream of doing; he asks for his share of the inheritance. Amazingly, his father consents to his request, and we may guess from various details of the story that such a share is considerable for the father is a wealthy landowner, able to afford his own hired servants. No sooner is the money handed over than the son cannot resist the call to adventure.

We may name it adolescence, but it is a characteristic which may occur at any time in our lives, a reckless pursuit of happiness. It happens when, on a sudden whim, the hard-earned savings are blown on the dream holiday of a life-time. It happens when the husband of a long-standing and happy marriage is drawn into an affair with a younger woman. It happens when the veil of excitement is drawn over the time-honoured foundation stones of our common sense. The father has given the son just enough rope to hang himself and the son quickly squanders everything that he has. Having demanded his freedom, he soon learns that life demands responsibility, which in itself requires reflection and hard work. Even so, he is too late in learning and finds that he is slowly starving to death; the excitement has never materialised, and the freedom remains a distant dream.

The saving quality, upon which the possibility of the whole story hangs, is the decision of the son to return home. It is a decision born more of good sense and calculation than of humility and repentance. Nonetheless, it is this single decision that creates the opportunity for the father to forgive and to reconcile. The son has nothing to offer except his labour for hire and his decision is to return home and become a hired labourer. But the father requires nothing beyond being afforded this opportunity to forgive.

This story is not just one of forgiveness. It is first of all a profession of the love of the father. He has never forgotten his son. He sees him while he is still a long way off, so we know that he has been constantly on the lookout for him. He runs to meet him and, embracing him, kisses him tenderly. There is no question of sanction or reprimand. He does not even want to hear the boy's apologies – he is just happy to have him home again. The past must now be forgotten, or at least, the time may come when the father and son will need to speak about the experience, but now is not the right time. From this moment the son is to have a new place in the household. He is given the best robe to show his dignity, the ring which denotes his authority, and he is the centre of rejoicing in the biggest feast of the year, for which the father gives the fatted calf. Reconciliation has gone well beyond forgiveness. The new relationship between father and son is far closer and healthier than it ever was before. The reason for the father's generosity is clearly stated in his own words, which reflect his compassionate love; the son that he thought had been lost has been found, the one who was dead has been brought back to life.

Then there is the other son. He is all too often overlooked when considering the parable. On the face of it, he is the responsible elder son who works hard and has none of that rebellious streak in him. He is probably someone of whom his father has always been proud. But this son has some disappointing characteristics. He seems to have no love for his brother. His brother's return is by no means a happy event for him. The strength of brotherly friendship seems to be missing entirely. He has no sense of forgiveness; rather there is the demand for retribution and petty justice. It is not fair that his brother should get away with his behaviour, let alone be honoured and welcomed on his return. There is no sense of reconciliation. He does not even want to go in to greet his brother. It is clear, too, that the relationship of the elder son to his father, though at first sight so admirable, is sadly lacking in love. He has never valued his father's generosity or recognised that he had claim not only to his share of the property but also to all that the father had. He has seen his relationship as essentially one of business and duty. On this basis, he apparently regards it as unsatisfactory because he has never been offered even a kid, let alone the fatted calf, to celebrate with his friends.

The story is so cleverly compiled that our sympathies may easily be changed, if not totally confused, as it unfolds. The younger son is a reckless and irresponsible character who is utterly self-centred. But he learns through a series of mistakes and becomes responsible and more mature. The older son, who has apparently always done the right thing, is later seen in his true light as judgemental, unloving and conceited.

The title to this chapter inquires 'Which son are you?' The answer is not easy to give because it requires a good deal of reflection and self-knowledge. We would all probably want to be the dutiful son on whom the father can depend, but surely not at the cost of becoming so pompous and unloving? None of us would be proud to be the younger son: reckless, irresponsible, selfish. To a certain degree at least we all have been him, which is disappointing and probably leaves us with a certain burden of guilt. But would not we all want to feel the warmth of love and forgiveness of the father, to experience the welcome of that home-coming, to be the object of such rejoicing? The younger son faced the fact of his own mistake and came home asking for a job. There is a terrible possibility that the elder son would be trapped forever in his own stubbornness and pride, unable to accept the generosity of the father's forgiveness, though equally in need of it. Characteristics of both sons are lurking within all of us. We should have no fear in discovering them, only in failing to make some progress towards correcting them.

The secret of this parable is that it not only invites us to look at ourselves as we have been and as we now are. It also beckons us to make something more of the time to come. The mistakes and failings of the past can be not only burdens which we insist on carrying with us, but also traps from which we find it impossible to escape.

The younger son looks as though he has learned from his mistake. He could, of course, have allowed himself to be trapped in his own stupidity, too ashamed to redeem his dignity. But we see him prepared to change and to go back to his father and to admit his mistake. He is thinking towards the future rather than being caught in the past.

The older son has possibilities, too. He has much to learn. He can let himself wallow in his resentment and sense of injustice. He can be angry both with his father and with his brother. Or he can begin to revise his ideas and learn that his attitudes in the past have been selfish and immature. He has much to discover about his father's love, and what it might be to love his brother. There is more to life than the greed that he has shown so far.

71

So it must be for us, as individuals. We make our mistakes and we have the opportunity to learn from them. We may ignore what has gone wrong, or we may challenge ourselves to see the error and discover also ways of avoiding its repetition.

PART 2

Preparation for the new rites

Chapter 8

The examination of conscience

The simple words of Christ, 'Follow me' (Mt 9:9), express the heart of the Gospel. They are, in a sense, the expression of what all our lives need to be about. Jesus was sent by the Father so that we might have the clearest possible image of the Father himself. Jesus' coming was the completion of his own self-revelation. But the coming of Christ was intended to be more than just allowing us the opportunity to glimpse the goodness of God. Jesus was to show us the way, a purpose which Jesus identified for himself in the Gospel of John when he said, 'I am the way, the truth and the life' (14:6). This, of course, cannot just be a statement which can simply be read and then left – it creates its own invitation. Jesus is the way and we must follow in that way.

That simplest and briefest invitation, 'Follow me', then takes on an enormous significance. If we are to accept it, it will mean setting out on a journey, a true pilgrimage, in which we will seek to be like Christ in all that we do, just as Christ was the mirror or image of God in all that he did. For the Christian, that pilgrimage began with Baptism, and it is strengthened and renewed by the power of the sacraments. Such a daily task is more than daunting. It calls us to nothing less than perfection. This is more than enough to absorb our full attention, but it is made even more difficult by the fact that, since our world is so different from that in which Christ lived, it is by no means clear, in every circumstance, how Christ would act now. The challenges then for us are twofold: to know what is right (Christ-like) in any given decision or action; and to put what is right into practice. This twofold invitation is the basis for our examination of conscience.

The dangers which may distract us are many, and we need to be clear what we intend by an examination of conscience and how we are to discipline ourselves to use it properly. We may get stuck with a very superficial image of Christ, one created through an uncritical reading of the Scriptures, or one based on childhood stories. We may find ourselves accepting simple codes of what is right or wrong which are simplistic, from a Catholic tradition which has not kept abreast with change. We may allow ourselves to be blinkered in such a way as to regard our own actions as purely personal, with few if any consequences outside of ourselves.

The true examination of conscience, however, reflects a growing understanding of who Christ was and what underpinned his life and ministry. It allows us to reach past simple rules and regulations, to question our decisions and actions, to see the consequences of what we do and do not do. It also prompts us to see that all our actions, however apparently personal or private, affect our relationship with other people and have a public quality in the context of a society in which every member has a part to play which will affect others.

It has to be said that the examination of conscience is not easy; that is, it is not easily done well. Like so many other expressions of our Christian faith, it will never be possible to say that we have suddenly arrived at the perfect use of the examination of conscience. As with prayer, it is something at which we must keep working without ever really being able to say what standard we have attained. While we cannot say that we can examine our consciences easily, or necessarily well, we can all begin somewhere and, while ever we are concerned to improve our self-understanding and are seeking to pursue that invitation to 'follow me', we may rest assured that our efforts are of very considerable value.

Let us look, briefly, at those three elements which are the means by which we will be able to examine our consciences before we attempt the examination itself.

It is so easy for us to romanticise and idealise about Christ. As children we all no doubt saw pictures of a young man teaching and healing – enacting the most popular episodes of his ministry, such as the sermon on the mount, the last supper, the entry into Jerusalem. Unless we attempt to become familiar with the Scriptures and reflect on the passages of the gospels, we will never come to understand what Christ was teaching and living for himself in the context of his own times. For the society in which he lived was full of turmoil. He was speaking primarily to Jews who were a nation under the occupation of the power of Rome. While they were waiting in eager anticipation for a messiah, they expected someone very different from Jesus. They expected a political hero who would restore the dignity of the chosen people by throwing the foreign soldiers out of their country and renewing the glory of Jerusalem and its Temple. It was a nation divided within itself with groups that differed in their religious expression. The Pharisees, Sadducees and Essenes were powerful groups whose views on faith had strong political overtones. The vigorous Greek and Roman religious influences further confused the culture and identity of the Jewish people. Economically life was not easy and was the constant prey to the elements and the seasons, and life itself was cheap.

It was in this context that Jesus was teaching. He had radical and challenging things to say to a nation which was hungry for justice. There was no sentimentality in his command to 'love one another'. To be able to love in such a hostile environment must mean that firm principles of truth, generosity, selflessness and compassion needed to be held. In order to say and do what he did, Jesus had to be utterly convinced about what was right at any given moment. There was no room for indifference or indecision – it was only a man of rock-solid principles of life who could sustain such a ministry and remain consistent even when it led to his death. There are moments in his ministry when it cost him dearly to remain, so uncompromisingly, with the truth.

Jesus was speaking about the need to eat his body and drink his blood. We are told that many of those who had been following him enthusiastically then decided that this was unacceptable and they went away. How easy, and how understandable, it would have been for him to compromise or to restate his teaching so as to entice the crowds to stay. But he lets them go rather than allow any compromise, and he asks his disciples if they will go away, too (Jn 6: 53-69). We can only begin to imagine the relief that Jesus must have felt when Peter said that there was no question of going away. Note that Peter did not say that of course he understood what Jesus was saying, and that his teaching was clear and utterly acceptable. Peter was saying, rather, that because he believed that Jesus was indeed the Messiah, he would stay, even though this teaching was difficult to understand.

Jesus was able to preach and to act so consistently because he was absolutely clear about the principles upon which everything he did was to be based. He would meet his critics, and his enemies, with truth no matter what the cost might be. And indeed the cost was ultimately life itself. If we are to follow Christ and to be – as we are called to be – 'other Christs', then our conviction must be as strong. We need, therefore, to know Christ. The very best way in which this may be done is to search for him in the gospels, to watch his behaviour, to listen to his words. As we grow in our knowledge of Christ, so we will grow in our own clarity of vision of what it is that we need to be doing.

Weighing our actions

There is a temptation to sit back and allow others to indicate to us what is right or wrong. As children we were constantly being told what was right and wrong by parents and teachers who wished to instil first principles as we grew up. So our first rules of life were in fact other people's, and the clearer and more general those principles, the easier they were to grasp. It was always wrong to tell lies, to steal or to be disobedient. While of course this remains true in general, we need to develop a sense of sophistication that will tell us that all lies are not the same, that there are different ways of being disobedient and indeed it is sometimes right to be disobedient. There is real danger that we merely catalogue whatever we do, and do not have any real perception about what it is that we have done wrong, to what extent it is wrong and, indeed, whether it is wrong at all. The catechism answers, that we may well have learned in our childhood and adolescence, may have been useful in their way, but there remains a more sophisticated picture which we must not ignore.

Much of this has been dealt with in Chapter 1 concerning weighing our faults, but it is important to see the measure of what we do, when we examine our conscience.

The public dimension of our actions

Events of recent years can leave no one in any doubt that incidents do not take place in isolation. The leak of radiation at Chernobyl threatened much of Northern Europe with a potentially fatal nuclear contagion. On the everyday scale, the industrial pollution of one country can, and does, have disastrous effects in others, as seen in the destruction of forests by acid rain and the pollution of the Mediterranean Sea. We have experienced the tides of economic and financial speculation which can drive down the economy of a nation. Such things happen on a global scale; how much more do the actions of individuals have a bearing on the life of a community.

We may consider that much of what we do is of a trivial and private nature. We may well have offended God, but we would not consider that there would, usually at least, be any repercussions on our neighbour. But this is not so.

Everything that we do has some bearing on others, on our community. Most things have a practical consequence. If I tell a lie, I lead people away from the truth. If I tell lies frequently, I may well undermine the quality of trust that someone may have in me and in others. If I steal, I offend the right of someone to own something and I break that fragile relationship by which people live in peace with one another, because I have introduced a reaction of suspicion and fear in the person from whom I have stolen. There may be practical effects even from the private thoughts that I have; my despising of others will surely be reflected in my behaviour towards them and in the way that I speak to others about them.

We must also remember that the things that we do wrong offend against not only our personal dignity (that of being made in the image of God) but also against the dignity of the Christian community (the Body of Christ). It offends, too, against the witness that I, as a Christian, will give to other Christians and to those who might only come to some knowledge of Christ through me.

Therefore, when we come to examine our conscience, we are not simply dealing with a list of things that have been wrong. The examination of conscience that we must seek is one which begins with a clear understanding of the values of Christ which need to form the basis of our lives. It needs to be a time in which I can evaluate what has gone wrong and why it was wrong – to see also the opportunities that have been missed and the lessons that may be learned from what has happened. It needs to be a proper evaluation of my life. Finally, this evaluation needs to be done in the light of other people around me who will have been affected, however indirectly, by my actions.

Chapter 9

The practice of the examination of conscience

There can be no single method by which we examine our conscience. Rather, as in prayer, we need to discover a way that suits us well and which assists us in coming to that sense of self-understanding.

Three things need to be borne in mind:

1. The examination of conscience is not something that is exclusively aligned with the Sacrament of Reconciliation. It can be useful to us on a daily basis and the findings merely given over to God in prayer, for the forgiveness that is so readily available whenever we ask for it. It may be something the fruits of which help us to celebrate more fully the penitential rite at the beginning of Mass. That said, it is clear that it should always be part, however remote, of our celebration of the Rite of Reconciliation. If we are sincere in seeking forgiveness and reconciliation with God, then our sincerity needs to be reflected in the preparation that we make for the sacrament. If we do not make some preparation, then we shall merely find ourselves repeating a familiar formula or shopping list which does not represent what we are at all.

2. Whenever we begin to scrutinise more closely what we are and what we may have done, we shall probably be very disappointed by what we see. I suspect that we all do things which – when considered carefully and objectively – will disappoint or even shock us. Did I really do that...? And so our very efforts to come closer to God may well

reveal to us that we are rather further from that holiness we seek than we had thought. At such a point it is vital to remind ourselves that this is in fact something of a blessing. How much better it is to discover who we are and to want to get things right than not to know about such things at all. Underlying our discovery and our discomfort is the certain truth that God loves us as we are, even though we may feel less good about ourselves. When we are reflecting on our lives and discovering things about ourselves, we are most certainly on the way forward and that, we may be assured, is most pleasing to God.

3. There is also an element of which we may all too quickly lose sight; that our examination of conscience should not simply dwell on what has gone wrong but be a reflection on what has been good. That, in its turn, must include not only those things which I have done well, but also an appreciation of what I have received. We can be very ungrateful. Surely we do not think twice about thanking a person for a gift that we have received; it is a matter of courtesy. It does not, however, always occur to us to be aware of all that we receive from God. We seem so often to take things for granted and even when we know we have received something, we perhaps do not give adequate time to reflecting on the fact. Our examination must be broad enough to be able to take stock of our lives as a whole, balancing both good and bad so as to better chart our direction and to establish our priorities.

I wish to mention three ideas which might help in building a practice of self-examination. The first method is the most straightforward, but I would hasten to suggest that it is not the easiest although it may be one which will be more rewarding later. It consists in merely being recollected and examining the events of the day, isolating the things that have gone wrong and perhaps recognising where opportunities to do more of what is right and good have been missed. I suggest that this may prove difficult simply because we tend to be uncritical about the events of the day.

For the most part we have lived through the day, reacting to circumstances and making decisions when they have been required. We tend to be locked in a sense of isolation from others. It is rather like people who try to learn a language on their own. They can read the books and do the written exercises; they can even attempt to speak the language if it has been written phonetically. But progress will be slow because there is nothing outside themselves by which they may measure their progress. To have a cassette of the language being spoken would be of great assistance in hearing the sounds, or to have a teacher who would correct the mistakes. Real progress will be made when there are individuals or materials outside the students by which they may check their ability.

The second method of examination, therefore, introduces this outside influence – the gospels. In this method, a passage of the Gospel is taken and the simple question is asked, 'Have I lived this today?' There are numerous passages in the gospels and in the Letters of St Paul which concern behaviour and all of them can be adapted so as to help us enquire about our lives. Take, for example, St Paul's great hymn to love in his First Letter to the Corinthians (13:1-13):

If I speak in the tongues of men and of angels,
but have not love,
I am a noisy gong or a clanging cymbal.
And if I have prophetic powers,
and understand all mysteries and all knowledge,
and if I have all faith,
so as to move mountains,
but have not love,
I am nothing.
If I give away all I have,
and if I deliver my body to be burned,
but have not love,
I gain nothing.
Love is patient and kind;

love is not jealous or boastful;
it is not arrogant or rude.
Love does not insist on its own way;
it is not irritable or resentful;
it does not rejoice at wrong,
but rejoices in the right.
Love bears all things,
believes all things,
hopes all things,
endures all things.
Love never ends;
as for prophecies, they will pass away;
as for tongues, they will cease;
as for knowledge, it will pass away.
For our knowledge is imperfect
and our prophecy is imperfect;
but when the perfect comes,
the imperfect will pass away.
When I was a child,
I spoke like a child,
I thought like a child,
I reasoned like a child;
when I became a man,
I gave up childish ways.
For now we see in a mirror dimly,
but then face to face.
Now I know in part;
then I shall understand fully,
even as I have been fully understood.
So faith, hope, love abide,
these three;
but the greatest of these is love.

In this passage, St Paul describes the quality of love,
and it is that love which is at the heart of all that we are
seeking as disciples of Christ. By using this text we can
begin to ask of ourselves whether we are indeed manifest-
ing the qualities of love in our own lives. One particularly

useful, and telling, thing to do is to take the kernel of the passage and to replace the word 'love' with our own name, i.e. 'John is patient, John is kind. He is not jealous', etc.

By this method we are prompted by the Gospel itself and we are asked questions by the text which perhaps we would not think of by ourselves. There are many other texts which may be used in this way.

Part of this second method, and perhaps a development of it, is to take just one word and search for it in all that we do. The word may represent something that is either good or bad. If it represents something bad, then we will be aware of where we have gone wrong and how many different expressions there may be of the same thing. Where the word we take is something good, we may see something of our progress or discover where we have missed opportunities to introduce this good thing into what we do. For example, if I take the word 'generosity', I may see first of all what I have done which has been generous. But then I will also discover perhaps that I am lacking in generosity in all sorts of ways: in the time I give to friends who need help, in the money I have given to the poor and to specific charities, in the way I have spoken to others or about others, in how I have prayed (particularly for those who may have asked for my prayers or who may need them) or the time I have given to God. With a little thought and reflection on events, we may well discover how many opportunities there have been which have been missed. This must not be allowed to be a time of despondency, but one of challenge and opportunity. Discovering the way ahead and planning how we may better respond to the call of the Gospel are part of the Christian life – vital elements of our pilgrimage.

The third method that I wish to propose here is the use of a purposely prepared text for the examination of conscience. It follows much the same principle as the employment of a Gospel text, namely, having something against which I may measure my behaviour. Just as there are many possible Gospel texts, so there are many such alternative texts which are readily available – or we may simply make our own. The advantage of this method is that such a text questions my life as it is, and reliance on the same text means that I am consistent in the questions that I am asking of myself and persistent in my desire to change. Many such texts are written as a prayer. I offer one such example:

Lord, I place before you my day/my week.
You know the value of any good that I have done.
You know, too, where I have not been Christ to others,
where I have chosen to please myself,
rather than to please you.
In these moments, guide me to discover
where I have gone wrong,
where I have missed opportunities,
where I can change.
Have I given time to you, in prayer?
Am I aware that all I do is done in your presence?
Have I asked you for my needs
or relied on my own strength and ability?
Have I witnessed my faith in you to others?
In my dealings with others ...
Have I been courteous, kind and gentle?
Have I sought to offer help to those in need?
Have I listened?
Have I maligned others with my speech, or thoughts?
Have I worked conscientiously for what I shall be
    paid?
Have I told the truth?
Have I been a source of tension in the home?
Have I assumed the goodness and work of others?
Have I thought of the needs of my family and others
    first?
In my own life ...
Have I been greedy?
Have I used the day well, or been undisciplined and
    lazy?
Have I taken proper rest and relaxation?

Such a list can be increased or decreased, tailored to our own needs; and it may end with a prayer, e.g.

Father, I thank you that you have shown me where I have not witnessed to your Son in my life.
Accept what has been wrong, given to you in sorrow, and forgive all that has been unworthy of you.
Guide me now to learn from what I see, and give me all that I need to put this new knowledge of myself into action in all that I do – so that all that I say and do may be worthy of you.

The examination of conscience is a tool for a work in building ourselves as Christians. It is good to be critical of ourselves and to know both what is good about the way that we behave and what is bad. The good may then be increased and enhanced, and the bad slowly corrected and transformed. It also allows us to create something positive even from the mistakes and faults in our lives. Our reflection on what has gone wrong may help us to equip ourselves more efficiently and so avoid repeating the fault in the future. We can grow in wisdom and knowledge of ourselves not only by the good that we do, but also from the experience of doing wrong, and learning. Nothing here needs to be wasted. If we are regular in our moments of examination of conscience, we will never be lost for the material that we wish to bring to the Sacrament of Reconciliation. We will have discovered, through our reflection, the priorities for our concern and where it is that we need first to be forgiven, and then to receive the strength and the power of the sacrament.

Chapter 10

Rite for reconciliation
of individual penitents

This is the form of the Rite which preserved and renewed that form of the sacrament which had been in use since the Council of Trent, and its roots are to be found in the twelfth century. It is the simplest of the three available forms and, working within an easy structure, it allows for a very considerable degree of freedom and spontaneity. The only people directly concerned are the priest and the individual penitent, and the only time that a third person may be present is when an interpreter is required because the penitent is either deaf or dumb or cannot communicate in a language known to the priest. Appendix II contains the text of this Rite.

This form of the sacrament remains the one which will be most familiar to many Catholics, and was the only form of the sacrament in existence in the years preceding 1977, when the new Rite was published. Its strength is to be found in the forum that it creates between the minister and the penitent in which a great freedom is allowed – giving both the penitent the opportunity to speak freely and express his concerns, and the minister the opportunity to respond in a very specific and appropriate way.

If this form of the Rite could be said to have disadvantages, they would exist in two specific areas. In the first place, it might be seen to over-emphasise a private sense of the sacrament in which the whole context is regarded as limited to the relationship of the individual with God, through the mediation of the priest and to the exclusion of all others. The other disadvantage lies in the lack of celebration and sense of catechesis. The individual is not being encouraged to prepare for the sacrament nor given any means to do so and, in contrast to all the other sacraments, there is no sense of liturgy and celebration. If this is the only form of the sacrament that a person undertakes, it may well become a rather stale experience, trapped by a routine and lacking any sense of innovation.

However, this was declared to be the normative form of the sacrament and one in which the penitent must have the right to anonymity, whether they should choose to use it or not. Because of the very nature of the circumstances in which the penitent comes to the priest, this form offers a sense of support in its atmosphere in which the penitent has the freedom to talk and to receive absolution and encouragement.

The Rite must be preceded by preparation both on the part of the priest and the penitent. We have already seen some methods by which the penitent may prepare through the examination of conscience. As the introduction to the Rite says, 'The penitent should compare his life with the example and commandments of Christ...' And it is important, too, that the priest should gather his own thoughts and recollect himself so that he may be better prepared to carry out this office which will include making an appropriate response to the needs of each individual in the celebration of the sacrament.

The formal commencement of the Rite is made in the welcome that each penitent should receive, the warmth and friendliness of which should reflect the joy of the reconciliation between the penitent and God which is about to take place. The making of the sign of the cross is the clearest reminder of what we are about: Christians seeking, through faith, to be part of the life and death of Christ, so as to rise with him to eternal life.

As the celebration begins, it is useful for the penitent to say a few words to indicate his or her state of life, and this can usually be done without compromising any anonymity that the penitent may wish to enjoy. Remember how helpful this may be to the priest who wishes to be part of the celebration and who hopes to be able to say something – however briefly – that may assist or encourage the penitent. Remember, too, that the priest may not investigate or probe into the life of the penitent: he may only ask those questions which sensitively seek to clarify what the penitent has said. So the few words spoken here may be most important in allowing the priest to find the context for what he may be able to say.

The final moment of preparation comes with the reading or reciting of a passage from the Scriptures, where time and the situation allow. This is a new element in the Rite of Penance, but its place is clear: our lives are guided by the precepts of the Gospel which express the standards of perfection to which we are called. They also remind us that the whole of God's plan of salvation has been directed to our conversion and reconciliation so that we may become heirs with Christ of the fulness of redemption.

There follows the central act of the whole Rite: the confession of sins and the act of penance or contrition. It is here that we have great freedom to express those things that weigh upon us. Into this moment goes the result of all our self-awareness and self-examination. And if we have been looking carefully at our lives, we will have been able to discover two or three areas of concern where the true values of the Gospel have not been reflected in the way we have behaved.

Realistically, this cannot be a time when we present an exhaustive list of every wrong. There is simply no time to do so, for all of us – no matter how dedicated we may be to living the Gospel – have any number of shortcomings. But it is in this part of the Rite that we may declare that we know we have failed, and particularly so in these two or three ways. Our examination of conscience may well have allowed us to see how a particular short-coming has in fact manifested itself in several different ways. For example, I may have realised that my shortness in speaking to a friend who came with a problem, my overspending on a holiday and my reluctance to stay late at work to finish a project, are all manifestations of a selfishness which now needs to be addressed.

It is to be hoped that the priest will be able to offer some help so that the penitent may be clear in his own mind what needs to be expressed, and especially that he will be able to put all that has been said into the context of God's love and his inexhaustible power to forgive. One of the greatest privileges of priesthood is to be called to act as an agent of such generous forgiveness and to be able, always and in whatever circumstance, to invite the penitent to 'begin again', with all the sins of the past removed.

The imposition of a penance is an essential part of the Rite, though it may sometimes appear to be trivial. Clearly, it cannot 'pay' for what has gone wrong, but it serves as a sign of sorrow for that and of a determination to be the stronger in the future. Many priests will ask that prayers be said for a penance, while on other occasions the priest may require a specific act of service, which the Rite reminds us 'will underline the fact that sin and its forgiveness have a social aspect'.

Finally, after the penitent's prayer which expresses both sorrow and a determination to begin a new life, the priest says the prayer of absolution.

The Rite itself points out that pastoral needs may curtail various elements of the sacrament. The essential elements needing to be retained in their entirety are the confession of sins, the acceptance of penance, the invitation to contrition and the absolution and dismissal. Indeed, references to appropriateness and circumstances underline the freedom and variation offered to both priest and penitent, and the Rite provides a number of alternative texts and prayers which may be selected according to suitability.

It remains clear, however, that no matter how much freedom and variety are offered, the success of the celebration and its value will depend on the two people who celebrate it on any given occasion. Such freedom needs to be delicately handled if the celebration of the sacrament is to be as positive and encouraging as we would like. Much will depend on the welcome of the priest and his invitation to the penitent to be at peace in the presence of God, and to receive forgiveness. Much, too, will depend on the penitent's confidence in reflecting on his or her life and feeling the freedom to speak about what is important. The sacrament which celebrates forgiveness and reconciliation can then become a most important element in the development and understanding of an individual's relationship with the community and with God.

Chapter 11

The new Rite of Penance

In December 1973, by a Decree of the Sacred Congregation for Divine Worship, a new Rite of Penance was promulgated. It realised in a practical form the decision of the Fathers of the Second Vatican Council that 'the rite and formulas of penance are to be revised in such a way that they may more clearly express the nature and effects of this sacrament'.

The new Rite was intended to serve two ends: to preserve the tradition of a sacrament instituted by Christ by which all people may be reconciled with God; and to promote, through the celebration of the sacrament, a fuller understanding of its essential quality. Rather than simply revising what was already in place in the form of the Rite for Reconciliation of an individual penitent, the Sacred Congregation broadened its scope of investigation and established two new forms of the Rite: the Rite for Reconciliation of several penitents with individual confession and absolution, and the Rite for Reconciliation of several penitents with general confession and absolution. It was hoped that this variety would cater more adequately for the needs of the Church throughout the world and for the needs of the individuals through a growing perception that individual fault and failing have a community dimension.

We will be looking at each form of the Rite in turn to consider their various strengths and weaknesses. But it is also necessary, at this stage, to consider briefly the Rite of Penance as a whole. It represents a most serious effort to renew a sacrament and to establish it in the life of the Church community. It was conceived within the context of the Second Vatican Council which, in its deliberations and documents concerning the liturgy, sought to strip away that which had become anachronistic and to rediscover each sacrament in the context of the early Church. This pursuit of the source called for a re-evaluation of the role of forgiveness in the ministry of Christ and its understanding and tradition in the life of the early Christian community.

In order for the fuller meaning of the sacrament to be understood and its value appreciated, it was thought particularly important to develop the sense of the community dimension of the Church while still preserving that individual and private element of an individual's unique relationship with God. The outcome has been the introduction of the three-fold form of the Rite.

To what extent might we say that the new Rite is a success? There is no doubt that the thinking behind the reform of the Rite was properly founded, and the establishment of the three Rites provides for a much more complete access to both the understanding and the celebration of the sacrament. But it would also appear that the new Rites have not had that full, and radical, impact that they deserve. There would appear to be three distinct reasons why this occurred.

In the first place, the initial introduction to the new Rite came at a difficult time. The Church community had been reeling under the very substantial changes in its liturgy, and in the new ways that it was finding for its expression of faith and doctrine. Although the doctrine remained the same, fundamental alterations were taking place in the way the Church expressed its self and its aspirations. While a most exciting time of challenge, it was also a painful period for many. For those reasons, perhaps, 1973 was not the time to introduce a new Rite of Penance. The fact that one of the three forms of the Rite was substantially the same as that with which people were familiar probably allowed the new Rite to be partially absorbed – almost by default.

This first difficulty, of unfortunate timing, gave way to the second. There seems to have been little enthusiasm to publicise the new Rite and to educate people in the exercise of it. The Sacrament of Reconciliation seems never to have benefited from adult catechesis. The seeds sown in the minds of children for their first encounter with the sacrament seem, generally speaking, to have been then left to mature or not. Certainly, some attempts were made, and the increasing occurrence of Reconciliation Services suggests that some progress has taken place. But an enormous effort is necessary to introduce a new teaching on a full sacrament, and so often time and opportunity are both lacking.

The final difficulty rests in the fact that, while the Sacred Congregation introduced the new Rite in three forms, the Holy See restricted the full use of all three. The celebration of the third form, with its general confession and absolution, is limited to a very narrow application. The confusion and indignation which have arisen over this will no doubt have reflected negatively on the general acceptance and implementation of the Rite.

However, as with all renewal, time is required for changes to be absorbed. It is to be hoped, with some degree of confidence, that time will indeed see an acceptance of the new Rite, combined with a clearer understanding and appreciation of the sacrament.

For those not familiar with the full form, *The Rite of Penance* is to be recommended. It sets out in full an explanation of each form of the Rite, enhances the text with suggested orders of service, and provides a wide selection of readings and prayers which may be used. To its credit, it is at pains to underline the freedom of choice in the celebration of the sacrament, emphasising that it should be tailored according to the needs and circumstances, and the time available.

Chapter 12

Rite for reconciliation of several penitents with individual confession and absolution

This form of the Rite represents a new departure. Those responsible for reforming the Rite did not wish simply to make superficial changes to the familiar. Having renewed the Rite for individual penitents, there was a need to enhance the whole concept of the sacrament and to make it of realistic assistance to the penitent. The theology of the sacrament had been lacking in its expression of the community dimension of reconciliation. An individual might be excused for thinking that the sacrament, as practised before 1973, had been concerned with a person's individual relationship with God; a question of repenting of what 'I have done wrong' in order to receive forgiveness from God. This was perfectly valid as far as it went, but there was no expression that an offence had been committed against the wider community of the Church, and that a sign and celebration of forgiveness should also be given and received in a public forum.

This is consistent with the view that sacraments are not private acts. The sacraments exist as the sign of God's love for his Church, the whole community, and any sacrament cannot become private property. Even when a priest celebrates Mass alone, for whatever reason, he celebrates it in the name of all the people. When a person is anointed, the whole community is offering prayers for the sick person. So it must also be with the Sacrament of Reconciliation. While the confession of the particular sin is maintained with the strictest confidence of the sacramental seal, the individual penitent still makes a public witness and renewal, and is reconciled with the community.

While that public sorrow is manifested at the beginning of each Mass, in a general way, it has now been established in the sacramental forum by this form of the Rite.

The emphasis of this form is that people should come together to recognise their privilege and place in God's Church, to remind themselves of God's purpose and his mercy and, in the context of prayer and celebration, to receive the forgiveness he longs to give.

This form of the Rite has become, in an increasing number of parishes, a regular part of the community's liturgy. Penitential Services, into which this form of the Rite is inserted, are to be found most commonly in Lent and Advent, liturgical seasons which the Church regards as most appropriate for the celebration of the Sacrament of Reconciliation, in preparation for the most solemn feasts of the resurrection and the nativity of the Lord.

Such a service may be constructed in any number of different ways, and *The Rite of Penance* outlines four different celebrations each of which follows a different theme. The good celebration will require planning, selecting a theme which is appropriate to the community in which the celebration will be held, and choosing hymns, music, readings and prayers which present and sustain the theme for all who participate. The Rite merely records an order of essential elements for the structure of the service: the introduction, the readings, the homily, the Rite of Reconciliation, and the dismissal of the people.

One practical difficulty that has arisen concerns how to maintain the momentum of a public service when individual confessions are being heard. Even when there are a number of priests, it may well take a considerable length of time to hear the individual confessions of a whole congregation, while those who have been to the individual confession must wait for the thanksgiving and prayers of the whole community before the dismissal at the end of the service. Music and readings can be usefully employed, but some silence needs to be maintained for those who are preparing for their confession.

The examples of Penitential Services given in *The Rite of Penance* offer a very good starting place for the preparation of such a service, and the volume also contains a large number of additional readings.

Chapter 13

Rite for reconciliation of several penitents with general confession and absolution

This form of the Rite of Penance is the most innovative, in that it does not require the individual confession of sins to a priest. There again, this form is not entirely without precedent both in the Old Testament establishment of the Feast of the Atonement and in the ministry of Christ himself who often forgave individuals without any confession of individual guilt. The early Church, too, included general repentance. In our own liturgy of the Mass, there is a general form of absolution at the beginning, in the penitential rite, albeit not the full absolution of the sacrament itself.

However, although an alternative form of the Rite, its use has been severely restricted; but the restrictions themselves are uncertain. The Code of Canon Law is clear that this form of the Rite should not be used unless certain conditions exist. The full canon states:

General absolution, without prior individual confession, cannot be given to a number of penitents together, unless:

1. *danger of death threatens and there is not time for the priest or priests to hear the confessions of the individual penitents;*
2. *there exists a grave necessity, that is, given the number of penitents, there are not enough confessors available properly to hear the individual confessions within an appropriate time, so that without fault of their own the penitents are deprived of the sacramental grace or of*

holy communion for a lengthy period of time. A suffi-
cient necessity is not, however, considered to exist when
confessors cannot be available merely because of a
great gathering of penitents, such as can occur on some
major feastday or pilgrimage.

(Can. 961)

The explanation is given in full in the introduction to the new Rite (nn. 31-35). It explains that 'individual, integral confession and absolution remain the only ordinary way for the faithful to reconcile themselves with God and the Church'. The principle has been clearly re-established, but the Rite must also be able to cater for particular and extraordinary circumstances and where there is a danger of death. People are not to be denied the sacrament merely for want of sufficient priests and for lack of time. Such particular circumstances could arise in mission territories, and in other places among other groups of people. However, the introduction is firm in stating that, where there are sufficient confessors, general absolution is not lawful just because there are large numbers of people.

It is for the bishop of the diocese, in consultation with other members of the episcopal conference, to establish when appropriate conditions exist for the use of general absolution. Further reasons may arise for this form of the Rite to be celebrated, and on such occasions the priest must seek permission prior to the celebration or, where this has not been possible, inform the bishop as soon as can be after the event.

There is also the condition laid upon the penitent, and explained by the priest, that where absolution is given to someone in grave sin, that person must go to individual confession before receiving general absolution again, and must do so within a year.

The sentiment of those who produced the new form of the Rite is clear: that there is a much preferred form of the sacrament which is to include individual confession, but the sacrament is still to be available where such individual confession is not possible. It seems to express a clear desire to make the forgiveness of God readily available.

However, some obvious anomalies arise. It is foreseen that this form of the Rite will be employed in missionary areas. Yet where it is employed, it is also very likely that there will never be an opportunity for an individual in grave sin to approach the priest for individual confession, even within the year. Furthermore, even in those countries which would not be considered to be missionary, it will surely be the presence of large numbers of people (and an insufficient number of priests for that occasion) which will require a priest to make the pragmatic decision to give general absolution. In an age where the use of the sacrament has declined, it would indeed be difficult to justify refusing people absolution because too many people came to receive it!

The value and desirability of this form of the Rite are still the subject of considerable debate. There are those who feel that individual confession, whether within the context of a penitential service or not, is an integral part of the tradition of this sacrament. It allows for an encounter with God through the mediation of the minister, which is evaded or ignored in general absolution. Considering the power of the absolution to forgive all sin, many would feel that general absolution offers a means to forgiveness which looks like an easy option or way out of the demands of individual confession.

It must be said that many would see strong arguments which would counter such criticisms. There are those who have returned to the sacrament because it is celebrated in this form, which offers then a sense of communal responsibility and gives value to a sacrament which had lost its meaning for them. For many the experience of individual confession has become irrelevant to the practice of their faith, while the opportunity to be reconciled with God within the context of the community offers a new dimension to their appreciation of what it is to be a member of the Church.

Predictably, the celebration of the Rite in this form

follows the Rite for several penitents with individual confession and absolution. The only variation lies in the fact that individuals do not have the opportunity to approach the priest for individual confession, and a special instruction is given by the priest in which he must explain to those present that if they are to receive general absolution, they need to be properly disposed to do so. This means that each individual must be responsible for repenting from their sins and be sure to resolve to turn away from them. They must also have the firm intention to make good any harm that may have been done through their fault and to make up for any scandal. They must also be sure to confess individually any serious sin that cannot be confessed in this liturgy. It is also for the priest to propose a penance for everyone, to which each individual may add something according to the circumstances.

Chapter 14

The short Rite

The inclusion in *The Rite of Penance* of 'The Short Rite' emphasises the flexibility of the sacrament and how it must always be seen and understood to be for people – to meet their needs. So great is God's desire that we be reconciled with him that the sacrament which seals our forgiveness must be immediately available and freely given in times of necessity and danger of death.

The short Rite is so simple that this availability is guaranteed. However, the arrangement and presentation of the new Rite also make it clear that the short Rite is not to be used merely as a matter of convenience. As a sacrament, the Rites must be celebrated with a suitable and befitting solemnity so that the value of what is being achieved may be properly appreciated. The short Rite is not, therefore, intended to serve as a short cut.

In times of necessity, particularly where there is danger of death, it is left to the discretion of the priest to confer the fulness of the sacrament with the greatest possible dignity in the circumstances which prevail. This may include elements of the full Rite, such as readings from Scripture, an examination of conscience and prayers, but it may also limit itself to the minimum, the shortened prayer of absolution.

Consistent with the principles surrounding the form of the Rite which includes general absolution, the person who has received this form of general absolution when in grave sin must make an individual confession when circumstances allow.

Conclusion

Apart from the very special privilege of celebrating Mass, I would consider the most important work of the priest, or of his priesthood, is to be an instrument of God's forgiveness through the Sacrament of Reconciliation. It is certainly a task that must not be taken lightly, for it touches the most fragile, and very often the most sensitive and damaged part of people's lives. A priest must always remember that here, as in all his priestly actions, he is an agent of God's love and forgiveness.

This forgiveness of God has qualities of perfection far beyond any human forgiveness. When we forgive each other, there is always the lingering possibility that, if a further offence is committed against us by the same person, we will want to unearth the past, and the second attempt to forgive will be all the more difficult. When God forgives, he wipes clean the record of all past sins and transgressions. It is as if they had never occurred. Once they are forgiven, all those sins are forgotten.

There is great sadness when people insist on dredging up the past, wanting to say sorry for things over and over again. That says two important things about them and their idea of God. In the first place, they do not really believe in the depth and the quality of God's forgiveness because they do not believe that they have received his pardon. Secondly, it means that they have continued to waste much of their energy on anxiety and worry about the past, and the mistakes they might have made and faults they have committed, and have therefore not been able to concentrate on living the Gospel today.

My experience, as a priest who has been working in a place where confessions are available every day of the year, has helped me to reach clear priorities about the celebration of the sacrament. There are certain elements which I would always hope to be able to communicate to those who come to confession.

It seems to me to be vitally important that a person knows that God truly loves them, just as they are. The very simplicity and completeness of the fact makes it hard to accept. That love has always existed and is a personal love for the individual. It is not a love which has to be earned; it would be well beyond our aspirations or our worthiness if indeed we had to earn it. Nor is it something which can be lost on account of our sins. Nothing can separate us from the love of God and, in a sense, that love is reinforced and all the more dynamic when we demonstrate our weakness. Christ told us that he came not for the healthy, but for the sick, and for the one who strays. So often people do not believe in such a love. They cannot accept it because it is so much more complete than the love that people have for one another, which is always limited by human weakness. Most people would admit that they have experienced the loss of love from other people when they have done something wrong, and they assume that God's love is lost in the same way. It is then easy to become afraid of God and to live in the anxiety that, because of sins committed, the love of God has changed to an anger and a desire to punish. This, however, is something that cannot be found in the way that Jesus speaks about the love of the Father.

When we have clearly understood that God's love is quite overwhelming and unending, then we can accept that a part of that love is the desire to forgive. Real love must look for reconciliation, which is a genuine and essential part of true love, even in its rather corrupted human form. God longs to forgive us and is impatient for us to turn to him for that forgiveness.

By believing in his love and forgiveness, we come to that maturity when we can look at our lives and accept all the disappointments that may be there because of what we do and the way we are. If we do not accept that God loves

105

us and that he longs to forgive, then the discovery of the bad things in our lives may well lead us to despondency and even to despair. We get caught in a sense of failure, which deepens when, no matter how hard we try, we cannot seem to put right what is wrong.

The next step forward in the sacrament is that desire to begin again. It must be the inevitable response to God's longing to forgive, and our sorrow for our own failings. This is the invitation which God makes in the sacrament. God's own words would, I am sure, be simple enough: 'I love you, I long to forgive you, I want you to start again'. That was the reaction of the father in the Parable of the Prodigal Son. It was also the reaction of Christ in any number of episodes in the gospels.

Sin is never to be the barrier in our relationship with God. It can always be forgiven. We make it the barrier by refusing to believe that it can be forgiven and by hanging on to it. Jesus was forever dismissing sin and simply encouraging the person to make a fresh start. If we do not feel that we are forgiven, it is because we have failed to forgive ourselves.

The desire to begin again should not be confused with the dream that all will suddenly be perfect. How wonderful it would be if, with all sincerity, we could approach the sacrament and ask that all our sins be forgiven, and never be troubled by those things again. That is not the reality. The journey to perfection is a slow pilgrimage of conversion. We will find that there will be certain things which seem to be stubbornly rooted in what we are – every desire and resolution to avoid them will fail. For some people, the necessity of often repeating the same material in confession leads them to brand themselves as hypocrites, asking forgiveness for something which, in all probability, will happen again. But God understands us and our weaknesses very well. He is not surprised by our all too consistent failures. But I suspect that he is rather less interested in our success in overcoming sin than in our determination to keep trying to put things right. It was, after all, that sort of tolerance which he showed to his disciples who were so slow to learn, and so quick to forget what he had taught them.

There is so much to celebrate in the sacrament. It should be encouraging and renewing. Being reconciled with God should be something that we look forward to, and which we experience with profound gratitude.

There are moments of great joy and emotion in the celebration of the sacrament. How humbling it is for the minister to hear people who are struggling to come closer to God – who refuse to give up even though they feel that they make no progress and are surrounded with problems and difficulties which to them seem insuperable. How moving to be with someone who unburdens their life with tears.

The purpose of the first part of this work was to consider our understanding of the Sacrament of Reconciliation. We had to acknowledge that the sacrament is far from being as popular as it used to be but that, simply because it is one of the sacraments of the Church and instituted by Christ, it is worthy of attention and reflection.

We have considered the value of the sacrament, and seen how, because of the way that it is taught initially to small children and little discussed in later years, it can stagnate. We have reflected on how it may better be used, what is required of those who use it, and the obstacles which need to be avoided if our use of it is to be beneficial. We have considered, albeit briefly, historical influences on the sacrament and the present law which is designed to protect its confidentiality and its availability. Hopefully what is written here may help individuals to recognise the Christ of the gospels in the forgiveness which is still offered in our own generation.

In the second part of the book, we have considered the new Rite of Penance which, while not providing all the answers, offers a new departure in our understanding of the sacrament and re-introduces a sense of freedom which may be expressed in three main forms. The new Rite offers a great deal, both in its theological presentation of the sacrament as one which is not merely celebrated between individuals and God but also within the context of the whole Christian community, and in the practical materials that it offers to the individual and to the community, for its celebration.

But it is also clear that, no matter how magnificent and edifying a document may be, it is necessary that individuals be introduced and educated in what the Church understands by the Sacrament of Reconciliation. With so many customs and traditions questioned and expelled in the critical storms of our own generation, it is more necessary than ever that members of the Church community know why this sacrament is so important and why it offers so much. Without good teaching even the most essential things of life and faith can be abandoned. In a radio programme broadcast in October 1992 a number of people were asked to comment on their experience of the sacrament. Few had little to say in its favour. Most had unpleasant childhood memories which had distorted its meaning and its place in the developing spirituality of the individual. Only one or two escaped what appeared to be a very prejudiced editorial team to express, somewhat clumsily, their happy experience and high regard for the sacrament in their lives. There remains much to be done to restore a sense of confidence. And the work is not primarily to be done for others – the starting place is the renewal of understanding in our own lives. I must know the importance for myself of the absolution that brings forgiveness and encouragement.

It seems to me that this study of a sacrament in the context of our Christian lives lived among others should not be allowed to come to an end without a further invitation being made. The final invitation for all Christians is, of course, to 'be perfect, as your heavenly Father is perfect'. There remains, therefore, the next clear step. It lies in a simple notion that is nonetheless radical if it can be grasped: if Christ calls us each day to the possibility of being forgiven, he also calls us to follow his example, and to forgive.

The matter is far too great to consider here at any length,

but it must not go unmentioned, since it forms the next link in our chain of progress. It is the next step in our own self-conversion, a further understanding of what it is to belong to a community of faith: the Body of Christ. If we are able to meditate on and recognise the incredible generosity of God's longing to forgive, then we must make that one further step and recognise that he calls us to forgive others.

There are many people who need our forgiveness – just as we need to be forgiven by many. People do hurt each other, whether they necessarily mean to or not. We will all have experienced this among our families and in the context of our lives. It may be that hurt is inflicted by people even when they are trying to do the right thing. There are also the hurts done through spite and selfishness.

We will all have our own stories of injustices received, opportunities denied. Jesus certainly had his own story of betrayal, lies and intrigue among those around him, even among his friends and chosen companions, who brought him to his own death. But at the hour of his death he had learned from the Father's forgiveness and he reflected that same forgiveness in his final prayers, 'Father, forgive them for they know not what they do' (Lk 23:34). It must be part of our discipleship to know the love of God and his forgiveness and to transmit that same quality of generous forgiveness to those who, by their actions, stand in need of forgiveness from us.

If, then, in these pages, you have come to glimpse something more of God's love for you, and the possibility – opportunity – of always being forgiven and beginning again, then that must be translated into the way we behave to others. Called to be Christ, we must forgive as intensely and completely as he did, always seeking to encourage others and to build them into that which we are all called to be – the Body of Christ.

Appendix I

The parable of the prodigal son
(Lk 15:11-32)

And (Jesus) said, "There was a man who had two sons; and the younger of them said to his father, 'Father, give me the share of property that falls to me.' And he divided his living between them. Not many days later, the younger son gathered all he had and took his journey into a far country, and there he squandered his property in loose living. And when he had spent everything, a great famine arose in that country, and he began to be in want. So he went and joined himself to one of the citizens of that country, who sent him into his fields to feed swine. And he would gladly have fed on the pods that the swine ate; and no one gave him anything. But when he came to himself he said, 'How many of my father's hired servants have bread enough and to spare, but I perish here with hunger! I will arise and go to my father, and I will say to him, "Father, I have sinned against heaven and before you; I am no longer worthy to be called your son; treat me as one of your hired servants."' And he arose and came to his father. But while he was yet at a distance, his father saw him and had compassion, and ran and embraced him and kissed him. And the son said to him, 'Father, I have sinned against heaven and before you; I am no longer worthy to be called your son.' But the father said to his servants, 'Bring quickly the best robe, and put it on him; and put a ring on his hand, and shoes on his feet; and bring the fatted calf and kill it, and let us eat and make merry; for this my son was dead, and is alive again; he was lost and is found.' And they began to make merry.

"Now his elder son was in the field; and as he came and drew near to the house, he heard music and dancing. And he called one of the servants and asked what this meant. And he said to him, 'Your brother has come, and your father has killed the fatted calf, because he has received him safe and sound.' But he was angry and refused to go in. His father came out and entreated him, but he answered his father, 'Lo, these many years I have served you, and I never disobeyed your command; yet you never gave me a kid, that I might make merry with my friends. But when this son of yours came, who has devoured your living with harlots, you killed for him the fatted calf!' And he said to him, 'Son, you are always with me, and all that is mine is yours. It was fitting to make merry and be glad, for this your brother was dead, and is alive; he was lost, and is found.'"

Appendix II

Text of the rite for reconciliation of individual penitents

RECEPTION OF THE PENITENT

Greeting

When the penitent comes to confess his sins, the priest welcomes him warmly and greets him with kindness.

Sign of the cross

The penitent makes the sign of the cross which the priest may also make.

In the name of the Father, and of the Son, and of the Holy Spirit. Amen.

Invitation to trust

Using one of the following forms, or other similar words, the priest invites the penitent to have trust in God:

< 1

May God, who has enlightened every heart,
help you to know your sins
and trust in his mercy.
Amen.

< *or* 2

The Lord does not wish the sinner to die
but to turn back to him and live.
Come before him with trust in his mercy. *(Ezek 33:11)*
Amen.

< *or* 3

    May the Lord Jesus welcome you.
    He came to call sinners, not the just.
    Have confidence in him. *(Lk 5:32)*

    Amen.

< *or* 4

    May the grace of the Holy Spirit
    fill your heart with light,
    that you may confess your sins with loving trust
    and come to know that God is merciful.

    Amen.

< *or* 5

    May the Lord be in your heart
    and help you to confess your sins with true sorrow.

    Amen.

< *or* 6

    If you have sinned, do not lose heart.
    We have Jesus Christ to plead for us with the Father:
    He is the holy One,
    the atonement for our sins
    and for the sins of the whole world. *(1 Jn 2:1-2)*

    Amen.

Revelation of state of life

At this point, if the penitent is unknown to the priest, it is proper for him to indicate his state in life, the time of his last confession, his difficulties in leading the Christian life, and anything else which may help the confessor in exercising his ministry.

LITURGY OF THE WORD

Call to conversion

Whenever there is an opportunity the priest, or the penitent, reads or says from memory a text of Scripture which proclaims God's mercy and calls man to conversion.

Alternatives

< 1

> Let us listen to the Lord as he speaks to us:

> 'See, today I set before you life and prosperity, death and disaster. If you obey the commandments of the Lord your God, if you love the Lord your God and follow his ways, you will live and increase and the Lord your God will bless you. Choose life, then, so that you may live in the love of the Lord your God.' *(Deut 30:15-16,19)*

< *or* 2

> Let us listen to the Lord as he speaks to us:

> I will give them a single heart and I will put a new spirit in them; I will remove the heart of stone from their bodies and give them a heart of flesh instead, so that they will keep my laws and respect my observances and put them into practice. Then they shall be my people and I will be their God. *(Ezek 11:19-20)*

< *or* 3

> Let us listen to the Word of God:

> The Lord is compassion and love, slow to anger and rich in mercy. For as the heavens are high above the earth so strong is his love for those who fear him. As far as the east is from the west so far does he remove our sins. *(Ps 103:8,11-12)*

< or 4

Let us listen to the Lord as he speaks to us:

Forgive your neighbour the hurt he does you,
  and when you pray, your sins will be forgiven.
If a man nurses anger against another,
  can he then demand compassion from the Lord?
Showing no pity for a man like himself,
  can he then plead for his own sins?
Remember the commandments, and do not bear your
  neighbour ill-will. *(Ecclus 28:2-4,8)*

< or 5

Let us listen to the Lord as he speaks to us:

Yes, if you forgive others their failings, your heavenly
Father will forgive you yours; but if you do not forgive
others, your Father will not forgive your failings either.
(Mt 6:14-15)

< or 6

Let us listen to the Lord as he speaks to us:

'It is not the healthy who need the doctor but the sick.
Go and learn the meaning of the words: "What I want is
mercy, not sacrifice". And indeed I did not come to call
the virtuous, but sinners.' *(Mt 9:12-13)*

< or 7

Let us listen to the Gospel of the Lord:

After John had been arrested, Jesus went into Galilee.
There he proclaimed the Good News from God. 'The
time has come', he said, 'and the kingdom of God is
close at hand. Repent, and believe the Good News.'
(Mk 1:14-15)

< or 8

Let us listen to the Lord as he speaks to us:

'Be compassionate as your Father is compassionate. Do
not judge and you will not be judged yourselves; do not

condemn and you will not be condemned yourselves; grant pardon, and you will be pardoned.' *(Lk 6:36-37)*

< *or* 9

Let us listen to the Lord as he speaks to us:

'What woman with ten drachmas would not, if she lost one, light a lamp and sweep out the house and search thoroughly until she found it? And then, when she had found it, call together her friends and neighbours? "Rejoice with me," she would say, "I have found the drachma I lost." In the same way, I tell you, there is rejoicing among the angels of God over one repentant sinner.' *(Lk 15:8-10)*

< *or* 10

Let us listen to the Lord as he speaks to us:

'If you make my word your home
you will indeed be my disciples,
you will learn the truth and the truth
will make you free.
I tell you most solemnly,
everyone who commits sin is a slave.
Now the slave's place in the house is not assured,
but the son's place is assured.
So if the Son makes you free,
you will be free indeed.' *(Jn 8:31-32,34-36)*

< *or* 11

Let us listen to the Lord as he speaks to us through his Apostle, Paul:

Give thanks to the Father who has made it possible for you to join the saints and with them to inherit the light.

Because that is what he has done: he has taken us out of the power of darkness and created a place for us in the kingdom of the Son that he loves, and in him, we gain our freedom, the forgiveness of our sins.
(Col 1:12–14)

A further selection of longer texts is provided at the end of this (Rite) in an Appendix.

LITURGY OF RECONCILIATION

Confession of sins and acceptance of satisfaction

Where it is the custom, the penitent says a general formula for confession (for example, *I confess to Almighty God*) before he confesses his sins.

The penitent then confesses his sins.

If necessary the priest helps the penitent to make an integral confession and gives him suitable counsel. The priest should make sure that he adapts his counsel to the penitent's circumstances.

The priest urges the penitent to be sorry for his faults, reminding him that through the sacrament of penance the Christian dies and rises with Christ and is thus renewed in the paschal mystery.

The priest proposes an act of penance which the penitent accepts to make satisfaction for sin and to amend his life. The act of penance should serve not only to make up for the past but also to help him begin a new life and provide him with the antidote to weakness. As far as possible, the penance should correspond to the seriousness and nature of the sins. This act of penance may suitably take the form of prayer, self-denial, and especially service of one's neighbour and works of mercy. These will underline the fact that sin and its forgiveness have a social aspect.

Penitent's prayer of sorrow

The priest then asks the penitent to express his sorrow, which the penitent may do using one of the following prayers or any other Act of Contrition which may be more familiar to him:

Alternatives

< 1

Remember, Lord, your compassion and mercy you showed long ago.

Do not recall the sins and failings of my youth.
In your mercy remember me, Lord, because of your
goodness. *(Ps 24:6-7)*

< *or* 2

Wash me from my guilt
and cleanse me of my sin.
I acknowledge my offence;
my sin is before me always. *(Ps 50:4-5)*

< *or* 3

Father, I have sinned against you
and am not worthy to be called your son.
Be merciful to me, a sinner. *(Lk 15:18; 18:13)*

< *or* 4

Father of mercy,
like the prodigal son
I return to you and say:
'I have sinned against you
and am no longer worthy to be called your son.'
Christ Jesus, Saviour of the world,
I pray with the repentant thief
to whom you promised Paradise:
'Lord, remember me in your kingdom.'
Holy Spirit, fountain of love,
I call on you with trust:
'Purify my heart,
and help me to walk as a child of light.'

< *or* 5

Lord Jesus,
you opened the eyes of the blind,
healed the sick,
forgave the sinful woman,
and after Peter's denial confirmed him in your love.
Listen to my prayer:
forgive all my sins,

renew your love in my heart,
help me to live in perfect unity with my fellow
    Christians
that I may proclaim your saving power to all
    the world.

< *or* 6
Lord Jesus,
you chose to be called the friend of sinners.
By your saving death and resurrection
free me from my sins.
May your peace take root in my heart
and bring forth a harvest
of love, holiness, and truth.

< *or* 7
Lord Jesus Christ,
you are the Lamb of God;
you take away the sins of the world.
Through the grace of the Holy Spirit
restore me to friendship with your Father,
cleanse me from every stain of sin
in the blood you shed for me,
and raise me to new life
for the glory of your name.

< *or* 8
Lord God,
in your goodness have mercy on me;
do not look on my sins,
but take away all my guilt.
Create in me a clean heart
and renew within me an upright spirit.

< *or* 9
Lord Jesus, Son of God,
have mercy on me, a sinner.

< *or* 10

> My God,
> I am sorry for my sins with all my heart.
> In choosing to do wrong
> and failing to do good,
> I have sinned against you
> whom I should love above all things.
> I firmly intend, with your help,
> to do penance,
> to sin no more,
> and to avoid whatever leads me to sin.
> Our Saviour Jesus Christ
> suffered and died for us.
> In his name, my God, have mercy.

< *or* 11

> O my God,
> because you are so good,
> I am very sorry that I have sinned against you,
> and with the help of your grace
> I will not sin again.

< *or* 12

> O my God,
> I am sorry and beg pardon for all my sins,
> and detest them above all things,
> because they deserve your dreadful punishments,
> because they have crucified my loving Saviour
>   Jesus Christ,
> and, most of all,
> because they offend your infinite goodness;
> and I firmly resolve,
> by the help of your grace,
> never to offend you again,
> and carefully to avoid the occasions of sin.

< *or* 13

> O my God,
> I am heartily sorry for all my sins,

because they offend you,
who are infinitely good,
and I firmly resolve,
with the help of your grace,
never to offend you again.

< *or* 14
God our father,
I thank you for loving me.
I am sorry for all my sins,
for what I have done and
for what I failed to do.
I will sincerely try to love you and others
in everything I do and say.
Help me to walk in your light to-day
and always.

Absolution

Then the priest extends his hands over the penitent's head (or at least extends his right hand) and says:

God, the Father of mercies,
through the death and resurrection of his Son
has reconciled the world to himself
and sent the Holy Spirit among us
for the forgiveness of sins;
through the ministry of the Church
may God give you pardon and peace,
and I absolve you from your sins
in the name of the Father, and of the Son,
and of the Holy Spirit.

Amen.

CONCLUSION

Proclamation of praise of God and dismissal

Alternatives

< 1

After the absolution the priest continues:

> Give thanks to the Lord, for he is good.

The penitent concludes:

> **His mercy endures for ever**.

Then the priest dismisses the penitent, saying:

> The Lord has freed you from your sins. Go in peace.

In place of the proclamation of God's praise and the dismissal, the priest may say:

< *or* 2

> May the Passion of our Lord Jesus Christ,
> the intercession of the Blessed Virgin Mary
> and of all the saints,
> whatever good you do and suffering you endure,
> heal your sins,
> help you to grow in holiness,
> and reward you with eternal life.
> Go in peace.

< *or* 3

> The Lord has freed you from sin.
> May he bring you safely to his kingdom in
>   heaven.
> Glory to him for ever.
> **Amen**.

< *or* 4

Blessed are those
whose sins have been forgiven,
whose evil deeds have been forgotten.
Rejoice in the Lord,
and go in peace.

< *or* 5

Go in peace,
and proclaim to the world
the wonderful works of God,
who has brought you salvation.

APPENDIX:

LITURGY OF THE WORD

If circumstances allow, the priest may choose a longer reading from
Scripture in place of the shorter readings provided (above).

The following are suggested:

Alternatives

< 1

Let us look on Jesus
who suffered to save us
and rose again for our justification.
Ours were the sufferings he bore,
ours the sorrows he carried.
But we, we thought of him as someone punished,
struck by God, and brought low.
Yet he was pierced through for our faults,
crushed for our sins.
On him lies a punishment that brings us peace,
and through his wounds we are healed.

We had all gone astray like sheep,
each taking his own way,
and the Lord burdened him
with the sins of all of us. *(Is 53:4-6)*

< *or* 2

Let us listen to the Lord as he speaks to us:

Treat others as you would like them to treat you. If you love those who love you, what thanks can you expect? Even sinners love those who love them. And if you do good to those who do good to you, what thanks can you expect? For even sinners do that much. And if you lend to those from whom you hope to receive, what thanks can you expect? Even sinners lend to sinners to get back the same amount. Instead, love your enemies and do good, and lend without any hope of return. You will have a great reward, and you will be sons of the Most High, for he himself is kind to the ungrateful and the wicked.

Be compassionate as your Father is compassionate. Do not judge, and you will not be judged yourselves; do not condemn, and you will not be condemned yourselves; grant pardon, and you will be pardoned. Give, and there will be gifts for you: a full measure, pressed down, shaken together, and running over, will be poured into your lap; because the amount you measure out is the amount you will be given back. *(Lk 6:31-38)*

< *or* 3

Let us listen to the Gospel of the Lord:

The tax collectors and the sinners were all seeking his company to hear what he had to say, and the Pharisees and the scribes complained. 'This man,' they said, 'welcomes sinners and eats with them.' So he spoke this parable to them:

'What man among you with a hundred sheep, losing

one, would not leave the ninety-nine in the wilderness, and go after the missing one till he found it? And when he found it, would he not joyfully take it on his shoulders and then, when he got home, call together his friends and neighbours? "Rejoice with me," he would say, "I have found my sheep that was lost". In the same way, I tell you, there will be more rejoicing in heaven over one repentant sinner than over ninety-nine virtuous men who have no need of repentance.' *(Lk 15:1-7)*

< *or* 4

Let us listen to the Gospel of the Lord:

In the evening of that same day, the first day of the week, the doors were closed in the room where the disciples were, for fear of the Jews. Jesus came and stood among them. He said to them, 'Peace be with you,' and showed them his hands and his side. The disciples were filled with joy when they saw the Lord, and he said to them again, 'Peace be with you.'

'As the Father sent me,
so am I sending you.'

After saying this he breathed on them and said:

'Receive the Holy Spirit.
For those whose sins you forgive,
they are forgiven;
for those whose sins you retain,
they are retained.' *(Jn 20:19-23)*

< *or* 5

Let us listen to the Lord as he speaks to us through his Apostle, Paul:

What proves that God loves us is that Christ died for us while we were still sinners. Having died to make us righteous, is it likely that he would now fail to save us from God's anger? *(Rom 5:8-9)*

< *or* 6

Let us listen to the Lord as he speaks to us through his Apostle, Paul:

Try to imitate God, as children of his that he loves, and follow Christ by loving as he loved you, giving himself up in our place as a fragrant offering and a sacrifice to God. *(Eph 5:1-2)*

< *or* 7

Let us listen to the Lord as he speaks to us through his Apostle, Paul:

Now you, of all people, must give all these things up: getting angry, being bad-tempered, spitefulness, abusive language and dirty talk; and never tell each other lies. You have stripped off your old behaviour with your old self, and you have put on a new self which will progress towards true knowledge the more it is renewed in the image of its creator.

You are God's chosen race, his saints; he loves you, and you should be clothed in sincere compassion, in kindness and humility, gentleness and patience. Bear with one another; forgive each other as soon as a quarrel begins. The Lord has forgiven you; now you must do the same. Over all these clothes, to keep them together and complete them, put on love. And may the peace of Christ reign in your hearts, because it is for this that you were called together as parts of one body. Always be thankful.

Let the message of Christ, in all its richness, find a home with you. Teach each other, and advise each other, in all wisdom. With gratitude in your hearts sing psalms and hymns and inspired songs to God; and never say or do anything except in the name of the Lord Jesus, giving thanks to God the Father through him.

(Col 3:8-10,12-17)

< *or* 8

Let us listen to the Lord as he speaks to us through his Apostle, John:

If we say that we are in union with God
while we are living in darkness,
we are lying because we are not living the truth.
But if we live our lives in the light,
as he is in the light,
we are in union with one another,
and the blood of Jesus, his Son,
purifies us from all sin.
But if we acknowledge our sins.
then God who is faithful and just
will forgive our sins and purify us
from everything that is wrong. *(1 Jn 1:6-7,9)*

The priest and penitent may choose other readings from Scripture.